super-cute
CROCHET

super-cute
CROCHET

over 35 adorable animals and friends to make

NICKI TRENCH

CICO BOOKS
LONDON NEW YORK

Published in 2009 by CICO Books
an imprint of Ryland Peters & Small Ltd
519 Broadway, 5th Floor, New York, NY 10012

www.cicobooks.com

10 9 8 7 6 5 4 3 2

Editor: Marie Clayton
Designer: Nicky Barneby
Photographer: Emma Mitchell
Stylist: Rose Hammick
Pattern checker: Susan Horan

A CIP catalog record for this book is available from
the Library of Congress.

ISBN-13: 978 1 906525 40 8

Printed in China

contents

Mrs Mittens

Pickle

Camilla

introduction

Tarquin

Mr Buff-Orpington

Vince

I used to be a bit nervous about making toys. In the past I always found it touch-and-go as to whether they were going to turn out cute or looking like something more akin to The Munsters' ugly cousins, complete with odd-shaped legs, lumpy faces, and drooping noses. After discovering this new way of crocheting toys I am now completely hooked and have found that it takes only a few essential guidelines to get the toys to look cute.

The style of these toys is loosely based on Amigurumi—the latest craze from Japan. These little cute projects are made using single crochet and crocheting in the round, which means you keep going in a spiral and don't get any join marks. It's essential when crocheting by this method that you use a stitch marker at the beginning of each round, otherwise you won't know when you've finished your round. There are lots of decorative stitch markers on the market, but I simply use a contrasting colored piece of yarn and loop it into the first stitch. When you get to the end of the round, simply hook the piece of yarn out and put it up to the first stitch again ready to start on the next round.

Most of the body parts are a tube or ball shape, which is easy for stuffing and you don't have any joining seams. This means that all these toys are ideal projects for either beginners or more experienced crocheters. Some of the toys use double stitches, but this is still a very basic stitch and very easy to accomplish with only a little crochet knowledge.

Creating the characters of each toy has been the most fun. From just a piece of yarn and a crochet hook it's amazing at how the toy can develop into such a personality. Each time I designed and made an animal I developed its character as it was being created, which made it easy when adding the detail and stuffing.

When you get to the stuffing stage, try to keep in mind the shape of the animal that you're making. It only takes a tiny bit of stuffing in a particular place on the head or body to give the character of the animal. For example, the koala has much more of a square-shaped head than other bears, so put a little more stuffing in to make rounded corners when stuffing its face. It's useful to find a picture of the animal in a book or downloaded from the Internet and to keep referring to it to get the shaping right.

Don't overstuff. You want the toys to be soft, squidgy, and cuddly and not like a hard ball. Don't put a lot of stuffing in at the same time as it will tend to mat up and become too hard—simply pull the stuffing apart and add just a little at a time, easing it gently into place. Using soft toy stuffing will give you the best result.

The wonderful thing about making these little cute toys is that they hardly use any yarn at all; they can be made with old scraps that need using up—or if you are buying yarn, you need less than one 50g ball of each color. I've made the toys in the book mostly using a Sportweight (DK) thickness of yarn, but Fingering or an Aran yarn would work equally well. Just remember to adjust your crochet hook size according to the thickness of the yarn: as a rule, a size B/1–D/3 (2.5–3mm) for fingering; D/3–F/5 (3.25–4mm) for sportweight; G/6–I/9 (4.5–5.5mm) for Aran yarn.

The hair on some of the toys can be a little time-consuming to make, but it's essential to spend time at this stage getting the shaping of the hair right. I usually work from the hairline first, getting the shape correct before filling in the spaces afterwards. Most of the hair is made by using the same method as for tassels. These are made by cutting a strip of yarn, folding it in half, threading the loop through the crochet with a hook, threading the tails of the strand through the loop and pulling to secure. It depends on how thick you need the hair—on most projects the hair has been made with single strands, but for thicker hair you can use two or three strands at the same time.

The eyes can be tricky. Always use safety eyes (I use The Craft Factory, ⅜in/9mm solid black eyes, ref CF047), which are completely safe if the toys are being given to children. Make sure that you line up the eyes before inserting the backs, so that the toys don't have a wonky look. If you prefer, you can embroider the eyes instead.

The equipment you need to make the toys is very basic; a crochet hook, wool, safety eyes, a wool sewing needle, and sometimes cotton thread and small bits of felt or fabric as embellishments and details.

I have included a couple of dolls in the book (Nicki and Dylan). They make the most fantastic gifts and I have made a doll for each member of my family, to give as a special Christmas gift. Customize your dolls to match your own family or your friends by adding some personal details—try changing the hair color or the hair style to match the person you are making the doll for.

I'm sure you'll find your favorite animal in the book. My family soon fell in love with most of them, particularly with Camilla the Pony and Dave the Lion, but my own particular love is for the Buff-Orpingtons from Kansas. We have a collection of real live Buff Orpington hens at home, along with a few ex-battery ones, all with their own particular appealing characters, and they keep us amused for hours. The Buff-Orpington crochet family is an immensely fun one to make and the Hatching Eggs take just an hour or two to come alive. When I was making these we had some real chicks hatch over the course of a couple of days and as each real egg hatched it was so exciting to imagine it might relate to one of the crochet eggs that were being born.

I have had so much unexpected pleasure in designing and making all the Cute Crochet toys—once you start making them you will very soon get totally engrossed and addicted. And the next thing you know you will have made all of the 35 patterns in the book, and all of their families too!

Cheryl

Boris

Andy

my family
and other animals

The Hatching Eggs are pipping, the Baby Chicks are all excited and Beryl the Bee has moved in to help out. Andy the Alien is landing later and word has it that he's brought extra cheese. Pete the Guinea Pig is having his hair cut (yet again) and Boris the Baby is having a few teething problems.

Beryl

Bruce

Saffy

Andy

Nicki

Nicki Trench lives in rural England with her two daughters, Pickle the Puppy (and a few more of his friends), the Buff-Orpingtons, Mrs Mittens and her daughter, Melody, Vince the Spider, Pete the Guinea Pig, the Sugar Mice, Cheryl the Snail, and sometimes, when he decides to show up, Ned the Goat.

materials

Head, Body, Legs, Arms: Wendy Mode DK, shade 203 (beige)

Shoes: Rowan Pure Wool DK, shade 039 Lavender (Lilac)

Mouth: Debbie Bliss Cashmerino DK, shade 05 (pink)

Eyelashes: Black embroidery thread

Hair: Rowan Pure Wool DK, shade 018 Earth (brown)

Necklace: Red beads

Bracelet: Clear beads

Headband: Ribbon

Dress: RYC Cashsoft DK, shade 509 Lime (light green)

F/5 (4 mm) crochet hook

Pair of safety eyes

Stuffing

abbreviations

ch chain; **rep** repeat; **sc** single crochet; **sc2tog** insert hook in st and draw up a loop. Insert hook in next st and draw up another loop. Yarn over, draw through all three loops on hook; **ss** slip stitch; **st(s)** stitch(es)

head

- Using beige, make 2ch, 6sc in second ch from hook.
- **Round 1:** 2sc in each st. (12 sts)
- **Round 2:** *1sc in next st, 2sc in next st; rep from * to end. (18 sts)
- **Round 3:** *1sc in next 2 sts, 2sc in next st; rep from * to end. (24 sts)
- **Rounds 4–8:** 1sc in each st.
- **Round 9:** *1sc in next 2 sts, sc2tog; rep from * to end. (18 sts)
- **Round 10:** *1sc in next st, sc2tog; rep from * to end. (12 sts)

Insert eyes and secure. Stuff head.

- **Round 11:** Sc2tog until opening is closed.

Fasten off.

body

- Using beige, make 2ch.
- **Round 1:** 6sc in second ch from hook.
- **Round 2:** 2sc in each st. (12 sts)
- **Round 3:** *1sc in next st, 2sc in next st; rep from * to end. (18 sts)
- **Rounds 4–12:** 1sc in each st.

Stuff body lightly.

- **Round 13:** *1sc in next st, sc2tog; rep from * to end. (12 sts)
- **Round 14:** Sc2tog around until opening is closed.

Fasten off.

Pin and sew body to head.

legs (make 2)

- Using lilac for shoes, make 2ch.
- **Round 1:** 6sc in second ch from hook.
- **Round 2:** *1sc in next st, 2sc in next st; rep from * to end. (9 sts)
- **Rounds 3–5:** 1sc in each st.

Change to beige.

- **Round 6:** Sc2tog, 1sc in each st to end. (8 sts)
- **Rounds 7–13:** 1sc in each st.

Fasten off. Stuff lightly.

Pin and sew legs to body.

arms (make 2)

- Using beige, make 2ch.
- **Round 1:** 5sc in second ch from hook.
- **Round 2:** *1sc in next st, 2sc in next st; rep from * once, 1sc in last st. (7 sts)
- **Rounds 3–10:** 1sc in each st.

Fasten off. Stuff lightly.

Pin and sew arms to body.

face detail

Embroider mouth and eyelashes.

hair

Cut several strands of brown yarn 8 in. (20 cm) long. Start at the hairline to make the shape of the hair and fill in with more strands at the back. Fold one strand in half, knot to head by pulling the loop through with crochet hook and threading tail through the loop. Make small stitches around head using brown yarn, to keep strands of yarn in place and to keep shape of hair. Trim hair to suit and cut bangs.

Tie and sew hair band in place. For necklace and bracelet, thread beads onto cotton thread and secure in place.

dress

- Using light green, make 30ch, ss in first ch to form a ring.
- **Rounds 1–4:** 1sc in each st. (30 sts)
- **Round 5:** Sc2tog, 1sc in next 14 sts, sc2tog, 1sc in each st to end. (28 sts)
- **Round 6:** Sc2tog, 1sc in next 13 sts, sc2tog, 1sc in each st to end. (26 sts)
- **Round 7:** 1sc in each st.
- **Round 8:** Sc2tog, 1sc in next 12 sts, sc2tog, 1sc in each st to end. (24 sts)
- **Round 9:** Sc2tog, 1sc in next 11 sts, sc2tog, 1sc in each st to last st, ss to first st. (22 sts)

Fasten off.

bottom of dress

Turn dress upside down, join yarn at start of round.

- **Round 1:** 2sc in first st, 1sc in next 14 sts, 2sc in next st, 1sc in each st to end. (32 sts)
- **Round 2:** 2sc in first st, 1sc in next 16 sts, 2sc in next st, 1sc in each st to end. (34 sts)
- **Rounds 3–6:** 1sc in each st, ending last round ss in first st.

Fasten off.

left shoulder

Turn dress right way up and work shoulders. With fasten off point on your right, join yarn in third st in towards the center.

- **Row 1:** 1sc in next 3 sts. (3 sts)
- **Row 2:** 1sc in next 2 sts. (2 sts)
- **Row 3:** Sc2tog. (1 st)
- **Row 4:** 1sc in st.
- **Row 5:** 2sc in st. (2 sts)
- **Row 6:** 1sc in next 2 sts. (2 sts)
- **Row 7:** 2sc in next st, 1sc in next st. (3 sts)

Fasten off.

right shoulder

Leave 3 sts free after left shoulder, join yarn to next st and work as left shoulder.

Try dress on Doll, pin and sew straps in place to back of dress.

Dylan

Dylan is passionate about skateboarding; he travels all around the country finding the best skate parks. He tried to be an emo, but didn't find wearing the eyeliner very comfortable. Instead he listens to grunge music like Nirvana and chilled out beats when he's relaxing with his friends.

materials

Head, Body, Legs, Arms: Wendy Mode DK, shade 203 (beige)

Shoes, Hair: Rooster Almerino DK, shade 202 Hazelnut (light brown)

Mouth: Black embroidery thread

Top: Rooster Almerino DK, shade 207 Gooseberry (green)

Shorts: Rooster Almerino DK, shade 205 Glace (light blue)

Underpants: Strip of fabric

D/3 (3 mm) & F/5 (4 mm) crochet hooks

Pair of safety eyes

Stuffing

abbreviations

ch *chain;* **rep** *repeat;* **sc** *single crochet;* **sc2tog** *insert hook in st and draw up a loop. Insert hook in next st and draw up another loop. Yarn over, draw through all three loops on hook;* **ss** *slip stitch;* **st(s)** *stitch(es)*

head

- Using F/5 hook and beige, make 2ch.
- **Round 1:** 6sc in second ch from hook.
- **Round 2:** 2sc in each st. (12 sts)
- **Round 3:** *1sc in next st, 2sc in next st; rep from * to end. (18 sts)
- **Round 4:** *1sc in next 2 sts, 2sc in next st; rep from * to end. (24 sts)
- **Rounds 5–9:** 1sc in each st.
- **Round 10:** *1sc in next 2 sts, sc2tog; rep from * to end. (18 sts)
- **Round 11:** *1sc in next st, sc2tog; rep from * to end. (12 sts)

Insert eyes and secure. Stuff head.

- **Round 12:** Sc2tog until opening is closed.

Fasten off.

body

- Using size F/5 hook and beige, make 2ch.
- **Round 1:** 6sc in second ch from hook.
- **Round 2:** 2sc in each st. (12 sts)
- **Round 3:** *1sc in next st, 2sc in next st; rep from * to end. (18 sts)
- **Rounds 4–12:** 1sc in each st.

Stuff body lightly.

- **Round 13:** *1sc in next st, sc2tog; rep from * to end. (12 sts)
- **Round 14:** Sc2tog until opening is closed.

Fasten off. Pin and sew body to head.

arms (make 2)

- Using F/5 hook and beige, make 2ch.
- **Round 1:** 5sc in second ch from hook.
- **Round 2:** *1sc in next st, 2sc in next st; rep from * to last st, 1sc in last st. (7 sts)
- **Rounds 3–10:** 1sc in each st.

Fasten off. Pin and sew arms to body.

legs (make 2)

- Using F/5 hook and light brown for shoes, make 2ch.
- **Round 1:** 6sc in second ch from hook.
- **Round 2:** *1sc in next st, 2sc in next st; rep from * to end. (9 sts)
- **Rounds 3–5:** 1sc in each st.

Change to beige.

- **Round 6:** 1sc in each st.
- **Round 7:** Sc2tog, 1sc in each st to end. (8 sts)
- **Rounds 8–13:** 1sc in each st.

Fasten off. Stuff lightly.

Pin and sew legs to body.

face detail

Embroider mouth.

hair

Cut several strands of light brown yarn approx 4 in. (10 cm) long. Start at the hairline to make the shape of the hair and fill in with more strands at the back and all around the head. Fold one strand in half, knot to head by pulling the loop through with crochet hook and threading tail through the loop. Trim to shape.

top

- Using D/3 hook and green, make 26ch. Ss in first ch to form a ring.
- **Rounds 1–4:** 1sc in each st. (26 sts)
- **Round 5:** Sc2tog, 1sc in next 11 sts, sc2tog, 1sc in next 11 sts. (24 sts)
- **Round 6:** Sc2tog, 1sc in next 10 sts, sc2tog, 1sc in next 10 sts. (22 sts)
- **Rounds 7–10:** 1sc in each st.
- **Round 11:** Sc2tog, 1sc in next 9 sts, sc2tog, 1sc in next 10 sts. (20 sts)

Fasten off.

left shoulder and sleeve

With fasten off point on your right, join yarn in third stitch in towards the center.

- ****Row 1:** 1sc in next 3 sts. (3 sts)
- **Row 2:** 1sc in next 2 sts. (2 sts)
- **Row 3:** Sc2tog, make 2ch. (1 st)
- **Row 4:** 1sc.
- **Row 5:** 2sc in st. (2 sts)
- **Row 6:** 1sc in next 2 sts. (2 sts)
- **Row 7:** 2sc in next st, 1sc in next st. (3 sts)

sleeve

- Work 10sc around straight armhole edge, ss in first sc.
- **Rounds 1–2:** 1sc in each st.

Fasten off**.

right shoulder and sleeve

Miss 4 sts after left shoulder and sleeve. Join yarn to next st. Work as for left shoulder and sleeve from ** to **.

Fit top onto doll and sew back of shoulders and sleeves in place.

shorts

- Using F/5 hook and light blue, make 20ch.
- **Row 1:** 1sc in second ch from hook, 1sc in each ch to end. (19 sts)
- **Row 2:** 1ch, 1sc in each st, 1ch, turn.
- **Row 3:** 1ch, 2sc in first st, 1sc in each st to last st, 2sc in last st. (20 sts)
- **Row 4:** 1ch, *1sc in next 3 sts, 2sc in next st; rep from * to last st, 1sc in last st. (26 sts)
- **Row 5:** 1ch, 1sc in next 13 sts.
- Ss in first sc to make a round for first trouser leg. (13 sts)
- **Rounds 1–4:** 1sc in each st.

Fasten off.

Rejoin yarn to first free sc of Row 4 and work second leg to match first.

Join back seam.

boxer shorts

Cut a strip of fabric to fit around hips. Hem and sew around doll. Pin shorts in place and sew to doll.

mrs mittens

Mrs Mittens is devoted to her daughter, Melody, and on weekends takes her all round the country to her ballet competitions. She was a prima ballerina in her youth and is very competitive. Once she even tried to trip up one of Melody's competitors backstage, but tripped over her own shoelaces instead!

materials

Head, Body, Arms, Legs, Ears: Rowan Pure Wool DK, shade 013 Enamel (cream)

Embroidered flower: Rowan Pure Wool DK, shade 038 Sugar Pink (pink), shade 041 Scarlet (red)

Muzzle: Pink felt

Nose: Black felt

Mouth, Whiskers: Rowan Pure Wool DK, shade 004 Black or black embroidery thread

Apron: Small piece fabric, ribbon

F/5 (4 mm) crochet hook

Pair safety eyes

Stuffing

Sewing thread to match felt

abbreviations

ch *chain;* ***rep*** *repeat;* ***sc*** *single crochet;* ***sc2tog*** *insert hook in st and draw up a loop. Insert hook in next st and draw up another loop. Yarn over, draw through all three loops on hook;* ***ss*** *slip stitch;* ***st(s)*** *stitch(es);* ***tch*** *turning chain*

head

- Make 2ch.
- **Round 1:** 6sc in second ch from hook.
- **Round 2:** 2sc in each st. (12 sts)
- **Round 3:** *1sc in next st, 2sc in next st; rep from * to end. (18 sts)
- **Round 4:** *1sc in next 2 sts. 2sc in next st; rep from * to end. (24 sts)
- **Round 5:** *1sc in next 3 sts. 2sc in next st; rep from * to end. (30 sts)
- **Round 6:** *1sc in next 4 sts. 2sc in next st; rep from * to end. (36 sts)
- **Rounds 7–8:** 1sc in each st.
- **Round 9:** *1sc in next 4 sts, sc2tog; rep from * to end. (30 sts)
- **Round 10:** *1sc in next 3 sts, sc2tog; rep from * to end. (24 sts)
- **Round 11:** *1sc in next 2 sts, sc2tog; rep from * to end. (18 sts)
- **Round 12:** 1sc in each st.
- **Round 13:** *1sc in next st, sc2tog; rep from * to end. (12 sts)

Insert eyes in place and secure. Stuff head firmly.

- **Round 14:** *Miss 1 st, 1sc in next st; rep from * until opening is closed.

Fasten off.

body

- Make 2ch.
- **Round 1:** 6sc in second ch from hook.
- **Round 2:** 2sc in each st. (12 sts)
- **Round 3:** *1sc in next st, 2sc in next st; rep from * to end. (18 sts)
- **Rounds 4–11:** 1sc in each st.
- **Round 12:** *1sc in next 2 sts, sc2tog; rep from * to end. (12 sts)

Fasten off. Stuff.

Pin and sew to head.

arms (make 2)

- Make 2ch.
- **Round 1:** 6sc in second ch from hook.
- **Round 2:** 1sc in each st.
- Continue until arms measure 1½ in. (4 cm).

Fasten off. Do not stuff.

Pin and sew to body.

legs (make 2)

- Make 2ch.
- **Round 1:** 6sc in second ch from hook.
- **Round 2:** 1sc in each st, continue until legs measure 1½ in. (4 cm).

Fasten off. Do not stuff.

Pin and sew to body.

ears (make 2)

- Make 5 ch.
- **Row 1:** 1sc in second ch from hook, 1sc in each ch to end. (4 sts)
- **Row 2:** 1ch, 1sc in each sc.

Rep Row 2 until work forms a square.

Fold square in half to make a triangle and sc sides together, at top point make 2sc.

Fasten off.

Pin and sew to head.

face detail

Embroider a flower below one ear.

Cut a felt oval for muzzle and a felt triangle for nose. Sew nose to muzzle. Embroider mouth detail and sew muzzle to head. Embroider whiskers.

apron

Cut apron from fabric using template, hem edges. Sew thin ribbon to top corners of apron and tie in place.

mr & mrs bertie buff-orpington

The Buff-Orpingtons live together in Kansas and are always very busy looking after their brood. Bertie first met Letitia when he answered an advert to partner her at a dance contest. They wowed the judges with their performance of the funky chicken and took home first prize. They are both keen singers and love to harmonize while having a dust bath in the herb garden.

materials

Head, Body, Wings: Artesano Hummingbird, shade Sunbird

Tail Feathers, Wattle, Comb: Rowan Pure Wool DK, 041 Scarlet (red)

Feet: Rowan Pure Wool DK, 034 Spice (orange)

Beak: Red felt

F/5 (4 mm) crochet hook

Pair of safety eyes

Stuffing

Sewing thread to match felt

abbreviations

ch chain; **hdc** half double; **rep** repeat; **sc** single crochet; **sc2tog** insert hook in st and draw up a loop. Insert hook in next st and draw up another loop. Yarn over, draw through all three loops on hook; **ss** slip stitch; **st(s)** stitch(es)

mr buff-orpington

body

- Make 2ch.
- **Round 1:** 6sc in second ch from hook.
- **Round 2:** 2sc in each st. (12 sts)
- **Round 3:** *1sc in next st, 2sc in next st; rep from * to end. (18 sts)
- **Round 4:** *1sc in next 2 sts, 2sc in next st; rep from * to end. (24 sts)
- **Round 5:** *1sc in next 3 sts, 2sc in next st; rep from * to end. (30 sts)
- **Round 6:** *1sc in next 4 sts, 2sc in next st; rep from * to end. (36 sts)
- **Rounds 7–14:** 1sc in each st.
- **Round 15:** *1sc in next 4 sts, sc2tog; rep from * to end. (30 sts)
- **Round 16:** *1sc in next 3 sts, sc2tog; rep from * to end. (24 sts)
- **Round 17:** *1sc in next 2 sts, sc2tog; rep from * to end. (18 sts)
- **Round 18:** 1sc in each st.

Stuff body firmly.

- **Round 19:** *1sc in next st, sc2tog; rep from * to end.
- **Round 20:** * Miss 1 st, 1sc; rep from * until opening is closed.

Fasten off.

head

- Make 2ch.
- **Round 1:** 6sc in second ch from hook.
- **Round 2:** 2sc in each st. (12 sts)
- **Round 3:** *1sc in next st, 2sc in next st; rep from * to end. (18 sts)
- **Round 4:** *1sc in next 2 sts, 2sc in next st; rep from * to end. (24 sts)
- **Round 5:** *1sc in next 3 sts, 2sc in next st; rep from * to end. (30 sts)
- **Round 6:** *1sc in next 4 sts, 2sc in next st; rep from * to end. (36 sts)
- **Round 7:** 1sc in each st.
- **Row 8:** *1sc in next 4 sts, sc2tog; rep from * to end. (30 sts)
- **Row 9:** *1sc in next 3 sts, sc2tog; rep from * to end. (24 sts)
- **Row 10:** *1sc in next 2 sts, sc2tog; rep from * to end. (18 sts)
- **Row 11:** 1sc in each st.
- **Row 12:** *1sc in next st, sc2tog; rep from * to end. (12 sts)

Insert safety eyes and secure. Stuff head firmly.

- **Row 13:** * Miss 1 st, 1sc in next st; rep from * until opening is closed.

Fasten off. Sew in ends. Pin and sew to body.

wings (make two)

- Make 13ch.
- **Row 1:** 1sc in second ch from hook, 1sc in each ch. (12 sts)
- **Row 2:** Sc2tog, 1sc in each st to last 2 sts, sc2tog. (10 sts)
- **Row 3:** 1sc in each st.
- **Row 4:** Sc2tog, 1sc in each st to last 2 sts, sc2tog. (8 sts)
- **Row 5:** Sc2tog, 1sc in each st to last 2 sts, sc2tog. (6 sts)
- **Row 6:** 1sc in each st.
- **Row 7:** Sc2tog, 1sc in each st to last 2 sts, sc2tog. (4 sts)
- **Row 8:** Sc2tog twice. (2 sts)
- Sc2tog.

Fasten off. Pin and sew in place.

comb

- Make 9ch.
- 1sc in fourth ch from hook, 5ch, 1sc in next ch, 4ch, 1sc in next ch, 3ch, 1sc in next ch, 2ch, 1sc in next ch, ss in last st.

Fasten off. Pin and sew in place.

beak

Cut a small diamond shape in felt. Fold in half lengthways, pin and sew in place.

wattle (make 2)

- Make 6ch, 3hdc in second ch from hook, 1sc in each of next 3 sts, ss in last st.
Fasten off.

Pin straight ends side by side at the top. Pin and sew directly under the beak. If the wattles are curling up too much, catch to body with a small stitch.

feet (make two)

- Make 7ch.
- **Row 1:** 1sc in second ch from hook, 1sc in each st to end. (6 sts)
- 1sc in next 2 sts, 4ch, 1sc in second ch from hook, 1sc in each ch, (first toe completed), ss in next st, 5ch, 1sc in second ch from hook, 1sc in each ch, 1sc in next sc, 4ch, 1sc in second ch from hook, 1sc in each ch, 1sc in last sc.

Fasten off. Pin and sew in place.

tail feathers (make 5)

- Make 2ch.
- **Row 1:** 6sc in second ch from hook.
- **Row 2:** 1sc in each st until tail measures 2¼ in. (6 cm).

Fasten off. Do not stuff. Pin and sew to body.

mrs buff-orpington

body

- Make 2ch.
- **Round 1:** 6sc in second ch from hook.
- **Round 2:** 2sc in each st. (12 sts)
- **Round 3:** *1sc in next st, 2sc in next st; rep from * to end. (18 sts)
- **Round 4:** *1sc in next 2 sts, 2sc in next st; rep from * to end. (24 sts)
- **Round 5:** *1sc in next 3 sts, 2sc in next st; rep from * to end. (30 sts)
- **Round 6:** *1sc in next 4 sts, 2sc in next st; rep from * to end. (36 sts)
- **Rounds 7–14:** 1sc in each st.
- **Round 15:** *1sc in next 4 sts, sc2tog; rep from * to end. (30 sts)
- **Round 16:** *1sc in next 3 sts, sc2tog; rep from * to end. (24 sts)
- **Round 17:** *1sc in next 2 sts, sc2tog; rep from * to end. (18 sts)
- **Round 18:** 1sc in each st.

Stuff body firmly.

- **Round 19:** *1sc in next st, sc2tog; rep from * to end. (12 sts)
- **Round 20:** * Miss 1st, 1sc; rep from * until opening is closed.

Fasten off.

head

- Make 2ch.
- **Round 1:** 6sc in second ch from hook.
- **Round 2:** 2sc in each st. (12 sts)
- **Round 3:** *1sc in next st. 2sc in next st; rep from * to end. (18 sts)
- **Round 4:** *1sc in next 2 sts, 2sc in next st; rep from * to end. (24 sts)
- **Round 5:** *1sc in next 3 sts, 2sc in next st; rep from * to end. (30 sts)
- **Round 6:** *1sc in next 4 sts, 2sc in next st; rep from * to end. (36 sts)
- **Round 7:** 1sc in each st.
- **Round 8:** *1sc in next 4 sts, sc2tog; rep from * to end. (30 sts)

- **Round 9:** *1sc in next 3 sts, sc2tog; rep from * to end. (24 sts)
- **Round 10:** *1sc in next 2 sts, sc2tog; rep from * to end. (18 sts)
- **Round 11:** 1sc in each st.
- **Round 12:** *1sc in next st, sc2tog; rep from * to end. (12 sts)

Insert safety eyes and secure. Stuff head firmly.

- **Row 13:** *Miss 1 st, 1sc in next st; rep from * until opening is closed.

Fasten off. Pin and sew to body.

wings (make two)

- Make 13ch.
- **Row 1:** 1sc in second ch from hook, 1sc in each ch. (12 sts)
- **Row 2:** Sc2tog, 1sc in each st to last 2 sts, sc2tog. (10 sts)
- **Row 3:** 1sc in each st.
- **Row 4:** Sc2tog, 1sc in each st to last 2 sts, sc2tog. (8 sts)
- **Row 5:** Sc2tog, 1sc in each st to last 2 sts, sc2tog. (6 sts)
- **Row 6:** 1sc in each st.
- **Row 7:** Sc2tog, 1sc in each st to last 2 sts, sc2tog. (4 sts)
- **Row 8:** Sc2tog twice. (2 sts)
- **Row 9:** Sc2tog.

Fasten off. Pin and sew in place.

materials

Head, Body, Wings: Debbie Bliss Rialto DK, shade 07 (yellow)

Comb, Wattle: Debbie Bliss Rialto DK, shade 12 (red)

Feet, Tail Feathers: Debbie Bliss Rialto DK, shade 11 (orange)

Beak: Pink felt

F/5 (4 mm) crochet hook

Pair of safety eyes

Stuffing

abbreviations

ch *chain;* ***hdc*** *half double;*
rep *repeat;* ***sc*** *single crochet;*
sc2tog *insert hook in st and draw up a loop. Insert hook in next st and draw up another loop. Yarn over, draw through all three loops on hook;* ***ss*** *slip stitch;* ***st(s)*** *stitch(es)*

comb

- Make 7ch, 1sc in fourth ch from hook, 3ch, 1sc in next ch, 3ch, 1sc in next ch, 2ch, 1sc in last ch.

Fasten off. Pin and sew in place.

beak

Cut a small felt diamond. Fold in half, pin and sew in place.

wattle (make 2)

- Make 4ch, 2hdc in second ch from hook, 1sc in next st, ss in last st.

Fasten off.

Pin straight ends side by side at the top. Pin and sew directly under the beak. If the wattles are curling up too much, catch to body with a small st.

feet (make two)

- Make 7ch.
- 1sc in second ch from hook, 1sc in each st to end. (6 sts)
- 1sc in next 2 sts, 4ch, 1sc in second ch from hook, 1sc in each ch (first toe completed), ss in next sc, 1sc in next sc, 5ch, 1sc in second ch from hook, 1sc in each ch, 1sc in next st, 4ch, 1sc in second ch from hook, 1sc in each ch, 1sc in last st.

Fasten off. Pin and sew in place.

tail feathers (make 3)

- Make 2ch.
- 6sc in second ch from hook, 1sc in each st until tail measures 2 in. (5 cm).

Fasten off. Do not stuff. Pin and sew in place.

Mrs Buff-Orpington has a real job on her hands looking after her large family. She is definitely free-range and organic and cooks only the very freshest ingredients, which she grows in the vegetable patch she keeps with Bertie.

hatching eggs

The Buff-Orpington Hatching Eggs will be ready to hatch in 21 days' time and the whole family is very excited about it.

lucy (pink): Gets sunburnt so she has to wear a hat. Today she has chosen her favorite flower hat.

lee (red): The rebel of the family. He's always mad and has a lot of tantrums. Last week he got his eyebrow pierced—he's definitely one bad egg. When he hatches he'd like to be a rapper.

monty (green): A thespian. He loves anything to do with the theater. When he hatches he'd like to audition for the musical *Joseph* and meet Andrew Lloyd Webber, the director.

violet (lilac): She is learning ballet and loves wearing a tutu. When she hatches she would like to join the New York City Ballet.

jack (blue): He's a skateboarder, this morning he fell off his skateboard and he has a sore head; Lee pushed him off, but luckily he was wearing a helmet and didn't crack.

saffy (yellow): She wants to be like her mother, because everyone says she looks like Mom. She'd like to be a farmer's wife and adores Ned the Goat, who used to live with them.

body

- Make 2ch.
- **Round 1:** 4sc in second ch from hook.
- **Round 2:** 2sc in each st. (8 sts)
- **Round 3:** *2sc in next st, 1sc in next st; rep from * to end. (12 sts)
- **Round 4:** *2sc in next st, 1sc in each of next 2 sts; rep from * to end. (16 sts)
- **Round 5:** *2sc in next st, 1sc in each of next 3 sts; rep from * to end. (20 sts)
- **Round 6:** *2sc in next st, 1sc in each of next 4 sts; rep from * to end. (24 sts)
- **Rounds 7–11:** 1sc in each st.

Insert safety eyes and secure. Stuff firmly.

- **Round 12:** *Sc2tog, 1sc in each of next 2 sts; rep from * until opening is closed.

Fasten off.

materials

Lucy (Pink)
Body: Debbie Bliss Rialto DK, shade 13 (bright pink)
Flower: Rowan Pure Wool DK, shade 039 Lavender (lilac)
Debbie Bliss Cashmerino DK, shade 25 (light green)

Lee (Red)
Body: Debbie Bliss Rialto DK, shade 12 (red)
Eyebrows, Mouth: Black embroidery thread
Piercing: Small silver bead

Monty (Green)
Body: Debbie Bliss Cashmerino DK, shade 25 (light green)
Hat: Debbie Bliss Rialto DK, shade 14 (light pink)

Violet (Lilac)
Body: Rowan Pure Wool DK, shade 039 Lavender (lilac)
Tutu, Flower: Debbie Bliss Rialto DK, shade 14 (light pink)

Jack (Blue)
Body: Debbie Bliss Rialto DK, shade 19 (light blue)
Hair: Debbie Bliss Rialto DK, shade 01 (white)

Saffy (Yellow)
Body: Debbie Bliss Rialto DK, shade 07 (yellow)
Bow: Red gingham ribbon

Scraps of yarn to embroider mouth
F/5 (4 mm) crochet hook
Pair of safety eyes
Stuffing

abbreviations

ch chain; ***dc*** double; ***rep*** repeat; ***sc*** single crochet; ***sc2tog*** insert hook in st and draw up a loop. Insert hook in next st and draw up another loop. Yarn over, draw through all three loops on hook; ***ss*** slip stitch; ***st(s)*** stitch(es);

lucy—flower hat

- Make 6ch, join with a ss in first ch to form a ring.
- 16sc in ring, joining tail in each sc round ring, ss in first st.
- *3ch, 1dc in next 2 sts, 3ch, ss in next st; rep from * 4 times. (5 petals)

Fasten off. Pin and sew to top of head.

Embroider center in green.

lee—eyebrows

Embroider eyebrows and sew bead in place.

monty—hat

- Make 2ch.
- **Round 1:** 5sc in second ch from hook.
- **Round 2:** 2sc in each st. (10 sts)
- **Round 3:** *2sc in next st, 1sc in next st; rep from * to end. (15 sts)
- **Round 4:** Working in back loops only: 1sc in each st to end.
- **Rounds 5–6:** 1sc in each st.
- **Round 7:** 2sc in each st. (30 sts)
- **Rounds 8–10:** 1sc in each st.

Fasten off.

violet—tutu and flower

Join yarn with ss in any st approx two thirds from top. Turn egg upside down. Working around circumference of egg, make 5dc in next st, *ss in next st, 5dc in next st; rep from *, ss in same st as join.

Fasten off. Embroider flower on Violet's head.

jack—hair

Cut several strands of yarn and knot through at top of head.

saffy—ribbon

Tie ribbon into a bow and sew to top of head.

face details

Embroider a mouth on each egg.

buff-orpington baby chicks

The Buff-Orpington chicks are called Quentin, Joaquim, Tarquin, Cosima, Tamara, and Arabella. They are being brought up in a very proper way; the girls will go to finishing school and learn how to cook properly and lay eggs in a lady-like fashion. The boys will learn to ballroom dance and avoid using fowl language.

materials

Head, Body, Wings: RYC Cashsoft DK, shade 509 Lime (light green)
Rooster Almerino DK, shade 203 Strawberry Cream (light pink)
Rowan Pure Wool DK, shade 039 Lavender (lilac)
Rowan pure Wool DK, shade 032 Gilt (yellow)
Rowan Pure Wool DK, shade 006 Pier (turquoise blue)
Debbie Bliss Cashmerino DK, shade 023 (apricot)

Beaks and Feet: Light pink, dark pink, bright green, lilac felt pieces

Combs: Rowan Pure Wool DK, shade 036 Kiss (red)

F/5 (4 mm) crochet hook

Pair of safety eyes

Stuffing

Sewing thread to match felt

abbreviations

ch *chain;* **sc** *single crochet;*
sc2tog *insert hook in st and draw up a loop. Insert hook in next st and draw up another loop. Yarn over, draw through all three loops on hook;* **st(s)** *stitch(es)*

head and body

- Make 2ch.
- **Round 1:** 6sc in second ch from hook.
- **Round 2:** 2sc in each st. (12 sts)
- **Round 3:** 2sc in each st. (24 sts)
- **Rounds 4–10:** 1sc in each st.

Attach safety eyes in place and secure. Stuff head.

- **Round 11:** Sc2tog to end. (12 sts)
- **Round 12:** 2sc in each st to end. (24 sts)
- **Rounds 13–16:** 1sc in each st.

- **Round 17:** Sc2tog to end. (12 sts)

Stuff body.

- **Round 18:** Sc2tog to end. (6 sts)
- **Round 19:** Sc2tog to end. (4 sts)

wings (make two)

- Make 7ch.
- **Row 1:** 1sc in second ch from hook, 1sc in each ch to end. (6 sts)
- **Row 2:** 1ch, sc2tog, 1sc in each st to last 2 sts, sc2tog. (4 sts)
- **Row 3:** Sc2tog to end. (2 sts)

Fasten off. Pin and sew in place.

comb

- 8ch, 1sc in fourth ch from hook, 3ch, 1sc in next ch, 3ch, 1sc in next ch, 2ch, 1sc in last ch.

Fasten off. Pin and sew in place.

beak

Cut a small diamond shape in felt. Fold in half lengthways, pin and sew in place.

feet (make two)

Using template, cut out four shapes. Sew together in pairs, leaving an opening for stuffing. Stuff lightly and stitch opening. Pin and sew in place.

beryl and the baby bees

Beryl is the grandmother of all bees. She is very kind and shares her honey with anyone who needs it. All the baby bees love her because she laughs a lot, tells them funny stories, and she wobbles when she flies. Everyone calls her Mama (pronounced marmar). The baby bees are very greedy and are trying to lose weight so they can fly faster. The baby bees are called Bella, Morella, Fin, and Luca. They live in a field quite near the Buff-Orpingtons and Ned the Goat.

head

- Make 2ch.
- **Round 1:** 6sc in second ch from hook.
- **Round 2:** 2sc in each st. (12 sts)
- **Round 3:** *1sc in next st, 2sc in next st; rep from * to end. (18 sts)
- **Round 4:** *1sc in next 2 sts, 2sc in next st; rep from * to end. (24 sts)
- **Round 5:** *1sc in next 3 sts, 2sc in next st; rep from * to end. (30 sts)
- **Round 6:** *1sc in next 4 sts, 2sc in next st; rep from * to end. (36 sts)
- **Round 7:** 1sc in each st.
- **Round 8:** *1sc in next 4 sts, sc2tog; rep from * to end. (30 sts)
- **Round 9:** *1sc in next 3 sts, sc2tog; rep from * to end. (24 sts)
- **Round 10:** *1sc in next 2 sts, sc2tog; rep from * to end. (18 sts)
- **Round 11:** 1sc in each st.
- **Round 12:** *1sc in next st, sc2tog; rep from * to end. (12 sts)

Insert eyes and secure. Stuff head firmly.

- **Round 13:** *Miss 1 st, 1sc in next st; rep from * to end. (6 sts)

Fasten off.

body

When changing color don't cut yarn, carry it up stripe.

- Using black, make 2ch.
- **Row 1:** 6sc in second ch from hook.
- **Row 2:** 2sc in each st. (12 sts)
- **Row 3:** *1sc in next st, 2sc in next st; rep from * to end. (18 sts)

Change to yellow.

- **Row 4:** *1sc in next 2 sts, 2sc in next st; rep from * to end. (24 sts)
- **Row 5:** *1sc in next 3 sts, 2sc in next st; rep from * to end. (30 sts)
- **Row 6:** *1sc in next 4 sts, 2sc in next st; rep from * to end. (36 sts)

Change to black.

- **Rounds 7–8:** 1sc in each st.

Change to yellow.

- **Rounds 9–11:** 1sc in each st.

Change to black.

- **Rows 12–13:** 1sc in each st.

Change to yellow.

- **Row 14:** *1sc in next 4 sts, sc2tog; rep from * to end. (30 sts)
- **Row 15:** *1sc in next 3 sts, sc2tog; rep from * to end. (24 sts)
- **Row 16:** *1sc in next 2 sts, sc2tog; rep from * to end. (18 sts)

Change to black.

- **Row 17:** Make 1sc in each st.

Stuff body firmly.

- **Row 18:** *1sc in next st, sc2tog; rep from * to end. (12 sts)
- **Row 19:** *Miss 1 st, 1sc in next st; rep from * until opening is closed.

Fasten off. Pin and sew to head.

legs (make 6)

- Make 5ch, 3hdc in second ch from hook, ss in each ch to end.

Fasten off. Pin and sew to body.

materials

Head: Rowan Pure Wool DK, shade 013 Enamel (cream)

Body: Rowan Pure Wool DK, shade 004 Black

Rowan Pure Wool DK, shade 032 Gilt (yellow)

Legs, Antennae: Rowan Pure Wool DK, shade 004 Black

Wings: Rowan Kid Silk Haze, shade 634 Cream

Mouth: Rowan Pure Wool DK, shade 036 Kiss (red) for Beryl. Rooster Almerino DK, shade 203 (light pink) for the baby bees

G/6 (4.5 mm) crochet hook (Beryl)

D/3 (3 mm) crochet hook (baby bees)

Pair of safety eyes

Stuffing

Note: *Use G/6 (4.5 mm) crochet hook for the Queen Bee. To make smaller bees, use either sportweight or fingering yarn and D/3 (3 mm) crochet hook, using same pattern.*

abbreviations

ch *chain;* ***rep*** *repeat;* ***hdc*** *half double;* ***sc*** *single crochet;* ***sc2tog*** *insert hook in st and draw up a loop. Insert hook in next st and draw up another loop. Yarn over, draw through all three loops on hook;* ***st(s)*** *stitch(es)*

antennae (make 2)

• Make 7ch, 2hdc in second ch from hook, ss in each ch to end.

Fasten off. Pin and sew to head.

beryl's wings (make 2)

• Make 9ch.
• **Row 1:** 1sc in second ch from hook, 1sc in each ch to end. (8 sts)
• **Row 2:** 2sc in next st, 1sc in each st to last st, 2sc in last st. (10 sts)
• **Row 3:** 1sc in each st.
• **Row 4:** 2sc in next st, 1sc in each st to last st, 2sc in last st. (12 sts)
• **Row 5:** 1sc in each st.
• **Row 6:** 2sc in next st, 1sc in each st to last st, 2sc in last st. (14 sts)
• **Row 7:** 1sc in each st.
• **Row 8:** 2sc in next st, 1sc in each st to last st, 2sc in last st. (16 sts)

Fasten off.

wing edging

Join yarn at start of first row.

• 1ch, 1sc in each row-end, 3sc in corner, 1sc in each st, 3sc in corner, 1sc in each row-end.

Fasten off. Pin and sew wings in place.

baby bee wings (make 2)

• Make 11ch.
• **Row 1:** 2sc in second ch from hook, 1sc in next 8ch, 2sc in last ch. (12 sts)
• **Row 2:** 1sc in each st.
• **Row 3:** Sc2tog, 1sc in next 8 sts, sc2tog in last 2 sts. (10 sts)
• **Row 4:** Sc2tog, 1sc in next 6 sts, sc2tog in last 2 sts. (8 sts)
• **Rows 5–6:** 1sc in each st.
• **Row 7:** Sc2tog, 1sc in next 4 sts, sc2tog. (6 sts)

Fasten off. Pin and sew in place.

face details

Embroider mouth.

Opposite: The baby bees love to read story books—particularly when they are about the daring adventures of dashing Dimble bee.

boris the baby

Boris plays a lot in the nursery and when he gets tired he sits in the pram. He always wears his bib because he dribbles a lot—he is teething. When he grows up he wants to be a politician because he likes to talk and he thinks they get to eat a lot in fancy restaurants and wear nice suits.

materials

Head, Body: Rowan Kid Classic, shade 850 Sherbet Dip (pink)

Hair: Rowan Pure Wool DK, shade 014 Hay (light brown)

Mouth: Pink embroidery thread

Bib: Rowan Pure Wool DK, shade 005 Glacier (light blue)
Rowan Pure Wool DK, shade 031 Platinum (light yellow)

Nappy: Rowan Pure Wool DK, shade 013 Enamel (cream)

F/5 (4 mm) crochet hook

Pair of safety eyes

Stuffing

Safety pin for diaper (optional—do not use if giving to a child)

abbreviations

ch *chain;* **rep** *repeat;* **sc** *single crochet;* **sc2tog** *insert hook in st and draw up a loop. Insert hook in next st and draw up another loop. Yarn over, draw through all three loops on hook;* **ss** *slip stitch;* **st(s)** *stitch(es)*

head

- Make 2ch.
- **Round 1:** 6sc in second ch from hook.
- **Round 2:** 2sc in each st. (12 sts)
- **Round 3:** *1sc in next st, 2sc in next st; rep from * to end. (18 sts)
- **Round 4:** *1sc in next 2 sts, 2sc in next st; rep from * to end. (24 sts)
- **Round 5:** *1sc in next 3 sts, 2sc in next st; rep from * to end. (30 sts)
- **Round 6:** *1sc in next 4 sts, 2sc in next st; rep from * to end. (36 sts)
- **Round 7:** 1sc in each st.
- **Round 8:** *1sc in next 4 sts, sc2tog; rep from * to end. (30 sts)
- **Round 9:** *1sc in next 3 sts, sc2tog; rep from * to end. (24 sts)
- **Round 10:** *1sc in next 2 sts, sc2tog; rep from * to end. (18 sts)
- **Round 11:** 1sc in each st.
- **Round 12:** *1sc in next st, sc2tog; rep from * to end.

Insert eyes in place and secure. Stuff head firmly.

- **Round 13:** *Miss 1 st, 1sc; rep from * until opening is closed.

Fasten off.

body

- Make 2ch.
- **Round 1:** 6sc in second ch from hook.
- **Round 2:** 2sc in each st. (12 sts)
- **Round 3:** *1sc, 2sc in next st; rep from * 6 times. (18 sts)
- **Rounds 4–8:** 1sc in each st.

Fasten off. Stuff body. Pin and sew to head.

arms

- **Round 1:** 2ch, 6sc in second ch from hook.
- **Rounds 2–5:** 1sc in each st.

Continue until arms measure approx 1½ in. (4 cm).

Fasten off. Do not stuff. Pin and sew to body.

legs

- Make 2ch.
- **Round 1:** 6sc in second ch from hook.
- **Rounds 2–4:** 1sc in each st.

Continue until legs measure approx 2 in. (5 cm).

Fasten off. Do not stuff. Pin and sew legs to body.

ears (make 2)

- Make 4ch, 1sc in second loop from hook, 3sc in next st, 1sc in final st, join with a ss in first loop.

Fasten off. Pin and sew to sides of baby's head.

face detail

Cut out felt round nose and sew on face. Embroider mouth.

Cut short strands of light brown yarn and loop through at top of head to create tuft of hair.

bib

- Using blue, make 5ch, join with a ss to make a ring.
- **Next round:** 2sc in each st. (10 sts)
- **Next round:** Turn, 1ch, 1sc in each st to end.

Fasten off.

bib edging and strap

Join yellow at one corner. 2sc in each st all the way round, ss in first st.

- Make 18ch or enough to go round baby's neck. Join with a ss onto other side of bib.

Fasten off. Slip over baby's head and sew in place at the back.

diaper

- Make 19ch, turn.
- **Row 1:** 1sc in each st. (18 sts)
- **Row 2:** 1ch, 1sc in each st.
- **Row 3:** 1ch, 1sc in each st.

Fasten off.

Rejoin yarn in sixth st along, make 1ch.

- **Row 1:** 1sc in next 7 sts, turn.
- **Row 2:** 1ch, 1sc in next 7 sts. (8 sts)
- **Row 3:** 1ch, sc2tog, 1sc in next 4 sts, sc2tog. (6 sts)
- **Row 4:** 1ch, sc2tog, 1sc in next 2 sts, sc2tog. (4 sts)
- **Rows 5–7:** 1sc in each st.
- **Row 8:** 1ch, sc2tog twice. (2 sts)
- **Row 9:** Sc2tog.

Fasten off. Pin and sew diaper in place.

boo boo, rebecca bear, and baby bruce

Boo Boo is an Australian bear from down under; he came over to America to experience life and fell in love with Rebecca Bear. Now he's trying to extend his visa to stay here longer, otherwise he'll be sent home and heart broken. Rebecca Bear is a model, but she's currently working as a receptionist in Chicago trying to save up enough money to go back to Australia with Boo Boo. They have a very happy baby, Bruce, named after Boo Boo's dad. Bruce loves cricket just like Boo Boo, but is learning to play baseball. His favorite team is the Chicago Cubs.

head

- Make 2ch.
- **Round 1:** 6sc in second ch from hook.
- **Round 2:** 2sc in each st. (12 sts)
- **Round 3:** *1sc in next st, 2sc in next st; rep from * to end. (18 sts)
- **Round 4:** *1sc in next 2 sts, 2sc in next st; rep from * to end. (24 sts)
- **Round 5:** *1sc in next 3 sts, 2sc in next st; rep from* to end. (30 sts)
- **Round 6:** *1sc in next 4 sts, 2sc in next st; rep from * to end. (36 sts)
- **Round 7:** 1sc in each st.
- **Round 8:** *1sc in next 4 sts, sc2tog; rep from * to end. (30 sts)
- **Round 9:** *1sc in next 3 sts, sc2tog; rep from * to end. (24 sts)
- **Round 10:** *1sc in next 2 sts, sc2tog; rep from * to end. (18 sts)
- **Round 11:** 1sc in each st.
- **Round 12:** *1sc in next st, sc2tog; rep from * to end. (12 sts)

Insert eyes in place and secure. Stuff head firmly

- **Round 13:** *Miss 1 st, 1sc in next st; rep from * until opening is closed.

Fasten off.

body

- Make 2ch.
- **Round 1:** 6sc in second ch from hook.
- **Round 2:** 2sc in each st. (12 sts)
- **Round 3:** *1sc in next st, 2sc in next st; rep from * to end. (18 sts)
- **Rounds 4–10:** 1sc in each st.
- **Row 11:** Sc2tog to end.

Fasten off. Stuff body firmly. Pin and sew to head.

arms

- Make 2ch.
- **Round 1:** 6sc in second ch from hook.
- **Round 2:** 1sc in each st.
- Continue until arms measure 1½ in. (4 cm).

Fasten off. Do not stuff. Pin and sew to body.

legs

- Make 2ch.
- **Round 1:** 6sc in second ch from hook.
- **Round 2:** 1sc in each st.

Continue until legs measure 1¼ in. (3 cm).

Fasten off. Do not stuff. Pin and sew to body.

materials

Boo Boo
Head, Body, Legs, Arms, Ears: Debbie Bliss, Rialto DK shade 05 (brown)
Nose: Beige felt
Nostril: Pink felt
Mouth: Black embroidery thread
G/6 (4.5 mm) crochet hook

Rebecca
Head, Body, Legs, Arms, Ears: Debbie Bliss, Rialto DK shade 14 (light pink)
Nose: Beige felt
Nostril: Pink felt
Mouth: Red embroidery thread
Beads: approx 25 red seed beads
Headband: Flower design ribbon
G/6 (4.5 mm) crochet hook

Bruce
Head, Body, Legs, Arms, Ears: Debbie Bliss, Cashmerino DK shade 07 (purple)
Nose: Beige felt
Nostril: Dark Pink felt
Nappy: Debbie Bliss, Rialto DK shade 01 (white)
Mouth: Black embroidery thread
Tie: Blue gingham ribbon
D/3 (3 mm) crochet hook

All Bears
Stuffing
Pair of safety eyes

abbreviations

ch *chain;* ***rep*** *repeat;* ***sc*** *single crochet;* ***sc2tog*** *insert hook in st and draw up a loop. Insert hook in next st and draw up another loop. Yarn over, draw through all three loops on hook;* ***st(s)*** *stitch(es)*

ears

- Make 2ch.
- **Round 1:** 6sc in second ch from hook.
- **Round 2:** 2sc in each st to end. (12 sts)
- **Round 3:** 1sc in each st.

Fasten off. Pin and sew to head.

diaper

- Make 19ch.
- **Row 1:** 1sc in second ch from hook, 1sc in each st. (18 sts)
- **Rows 2–3:** 1ch, 1sc in each st.

Fasten off.

Rejoin yarn to sixth st along.

- **Rows 4–5:** 1ch, 1sc in next 8 sts, turn.
- **Row 6:** 1ch, sc2tog, 1sc in next 4 sts, sc2tog. (6 sts)
- **Row 7:** 1ch, sc2tog, 1sc in next 2 sts, sc2tog. (4 sts)
- **Rows 8–10:** 1sc in each st.
- **Row 11:** 1ch, sc2tog twice. (2 sts)
- **Row 12:** Sc2tog.

Fasten off.

face detail

Cut a felt circle for muzzle. Cut a small felt oval for nose and sew onto muzzle. Embroider mouth. Sew muzzle on face.

rebecca bear

Thread beads onto some thread and tie and sew in place at the back. Place ribbon around head and tie a bow at the front. Trim ends, pin and sew in place.

baby bear

Make a tie knot using ribbon around neck. Pin and sew diaper in place.

Opposite: Boo Boo and Rebecca are blissfully happy together in Chicago—but worry that Boo Boo may have to go back to Oz if his visa runs out.

andy the alien

Andy came to Earth because they don't have cheese on his planet; he loves cheese but he's only ever tasted cheddar. He loves animals and recently decided to go vegetarian so doesn't eat meat, and his eyesight is very good because he eats lots of carrots. Sometimes he gets hayfever, which makes his eyes go the same color as the carrots.

materials

Head, Body: Rooster Almerino DK, shade 207 Gooseberry (green)

Legs: Rooster Almerino DK, shade 205 Glace (light blue)

Hair: RYC Cashsoft DK, shade 503 Mirage (mid blue)

Ears: Rooster Almerino DK, shade 203 Strawberry Cream (light pink)

Mouth: RYC Cashsoft DK, shade 519 Black, Red felt

Eyes: Orange felt

F/5 (4 mm) crochet hook

Three safety eyes

Stuffing

abbreviations

ch *chain;* **rep** *repeat;* **sc** *single crochet;* **sc2tog** *insert hook in st and draw up a loop. Insert hook in next st and draw up another loop. Yarn over, draw through all three loops on hook;* **ss** *slip stitch;* **st(s)** *stitch(es)*

head

- Make 2ch.
- **Round 1:** 6sc in second ch from hook.
- **Round 2:** 2sc in each st. (12 sts)
- **Round 3:** *1sc in next st, 2sc in next st; rep from * to end. (18 sts)
- **Round 4:** *1sc in next 2 sts, 2sc in next st; rep from * to end. (24 sts)
- **Round 5:** *1sc in next 3 sts, 2sc in next st; rep from * to end. (30 sts)
- **Round 6:** *1sc in next 4 sts, 2sc in next st; rep from * to end. (36 sts)
- **Round 7:** 1sc in each st.
- **Round 8:** *1sc in next 4 sts, sc2tog; rep from * to end. (30 sts)
- **Round 9:** *1sc in next 3 sts, sc2tog; rep from * to end. (24 sts)
- **Round 10:** *1sc in next 2 sts, sc2tog; rep from * to end. (18 sts)
- **Round 11:** Make 1sc in each st.

Cut out three small round circles of felt, make a small hole in the center of each circle and insert safety eye through each. Insert in Alien's head in position and secure. Sew felt to head with sewing thread.

Stuff head firmly.

- **Round 12:** *1sc in next st, sc2tog; rep from * to end. (12 sts)
- **Round 13:** *Miss 1st, 1sc in next st; rep from * until opening is closed.

Fasten off.

body

- Make 2ch.
- **Round 1:** 6sc in second ch from hook.
- **Round 2:** 2sc in each st. (12 sts)
- **Round 3:** *1sc in next st, 2sc in next st; rep from * to end. (18 sts)
- **Rounds 4–10:** 1sc in each st.
- **Round 11:** Sc2tog to end.

Fasten off. Stuff firmly.

Pin and sew to head.

legs (make 6)

- Make 2ch.
- **Round 1:** 6sc in second ch from hook.
- **Round 2:** 1sc in each st.

Continue until leg measures 1½ in. (4 cm).

Fasten off. Do not stuff.

Pin and sew to body.

ears

- Make 6ch
- **Row 1:** 2sc in second st from hook, 1sc in next 3ch, 2sc in last st, turn. (7 sts)
- **Row 2:** 1sc in each st.
- **Row 3:** Sc2tog, 1sc in next 3 sts, sc2tog. (5 sts)
- **Row 4:** Sc2tog, 1sc in next st, sc2tog. (3 sts)

Fasten off. With last row to head, pin and sew in place.

hair

- Make 7ch.
- Ss in second ch from hook, *4ch, miss first of these ch, ss in each of next 3ch, ss in next ch along original ch; rep from * to end until you have five spikes.

Fasten off.

Sew along top of head lengthways so spikes stick up.

face detail

Embroider mouth with black yarn, cut out tongue-shaped felt and sew in place just under mouth.

down on the farm

Come and meet Camilla the Pony and all her friends down at Super Cute Farm. You'll find the Two Little Pigs making jam, the Sugar Mice causing havoc and Pickle the Puppy practicing for the Olympics. Don't forget your rubber boots—and don't tread on Cheryl as you arrive.

Tiggy

Daisy

Camilla

Ned

camilla the pretty pony

Camilla is very pretty and her favorite color is pink. She is very clever and has won first prize at the local gymkhana in the class for "The Pony The Judge Would Most Like To Own." She loves running in the meadow with no tack so she can feel the breeze between her ears. She is an actress and has starred in lots of famous films.

head

- Make 2ch.
- **Round 1:** 6sc in second ch from hook.
- **Round 2:** 2sc in each st. (12 sts)
- **Rounds 3–7:** 1sc in each st.
- **Round 8:** 1sc in each of next 3 sts, 2sc in each of next 6 sts, 1sc in each of last 3 sts. (18 sts)
- **Round 9:** 1sc in each st.
- **Round 10:** 1sc in each of first 6 sts, 2sc in each of next 6 sts, 1sc in each of last 6 sts. (24 sts)
- **Rounds 11–14:** 1sc in each st.
- **Round 15:** *1sc in next 2 sts, sc2tog; rep from * to end. (18 sts)

Insert eyes and secure. Stuff head.

- **Round 16:** *1sc in next st, sc2tog; rep from * to end. (12 sts)
- **Round 17:** *sc2tog; rep from * to end. (6 sts)

Fasten off.

neck

- Make 18ch, ss in first ch to form a ring.
- **Round 1:** 1ch, 1sc in each ch to end.
- **Rounds 2–6:** 1sc in each st.
- **Rounds 7–8:** Ss in first 9 sts, 1sc in each of last 9 sts.

Fasten off. Stuff.

Pin and sew to back of head with shaped edge at top.

ears (make 2)

- Make 4ch.
- 1sc in second ch from hook, 1sc in next ch, 3sc in last ch.

Work in other side of ch.

- 1sc in next 2 sts, ss in first sc.

Fasten off. Pin and sew in place.

body

- Make 2ch.
- **Round 1:** 6sc in second ch from hook.
- **Round 2:** 2sc in each st. (12 sts)
- **Round 3:** *1sc in next st, 2sc in next st; rep from * to end of round. (18 sts)
- **Round 4:** *1sc in next 2 sts, 2sc in next st; rep from * to end of round. (24 sts)
- **Rounds 5–14:** 1sc in each st.
- **Round 15:** 1sc in first 6 sts, 2sc in each of the next 12 sts, 1sc in last 6 sts.
- **Rounds 16–19:** 1sc in each st.
- **Round 20:** *1sc in next 4 sts, sc2tog; rep from * to end. (30 sts)
- **Round 21:** *1sc in next 3 sts, sc2tog; rep from * to end. (24 sts)
- **Round 22:** *1sc in next 2 sts, sc2tog; rep from * to end. (18 sts)
- **Round 23:** *1sc in next st, sc2tog; rep from * to end. (12 sts)

Stuff body.

- **Round 24:** Sc2tog around until opening is closed.

Fasten off. Pin and sew in place to neck.

materials

Head, Neck, Body, Legs: Rooster Almerino DK, shade 201 Cornish (cream)

Rooster Almerino DK, shade 202 Hazlenut (light brown)

Headcollar: Rooster Almerino Aran, shade 302 Sugared Almond (blue)

Mane, Tail: RYC Cashsoft DK, shade 520 Bloom (pink)

Red rose motif

Red gingham ribbon

F/5 (4 mm) crochet hook

Pair of safety eyes

Stuffing

abbreviations

ch *chain;* ***sc*** *single crochet;* ***sc2tog*** *insert hook in st and draw up a loop. Insert hook in next st and draw up another loop. Yarn over, draw through all three loops on hook;* ***rep*** *repeat;* ***ss*** *slip stitch;* ***st(s)*** *stitch(es)*

legs (make 4)

- Using light brown for hooves, make 2ch.
- **Round 1:** 6sc in second ch from hook.
- **Round 2:** 2sc in each st. (12 sts)
- **Round 3:** *1sc in next st, 2sc in next st; rep from * to end. (18 sts)
- **Round 4:** 1sc in the back of each st.

Change to cream for leg.

- **Round 5:** 1sc in each st.
- **Round 6:** *1sc in next st, sc2tog; rep from * to end of round. (12 sts)
- **Rounds 7–19:** 1sc in each st.
- **Round 20:** *Sc2tog; rep from * to end. (6 sts)

Fasten off. Stuff legs. Pin and sew to body.

forelock and mane

Cut lengths of pink 8 in. (20 cm) long. Using crochet hook, hook strands to form a loop and thread through to secure, two at a time, through top of head at the front for forelock and down one side of the neck just left of center. Trim.

tail

Cut fifteen lengths of pink 10½ in. (26 cm) long. Attach to rear end of body.

Tie ribbon to top of tail.

headcollar

Join blue yarn underneath pony's head at join to neck.

- Make 30ch, or enough chains to go round pony's head behind the ears. Join with a ss at start of ch.
- Make 5ch towards front, approx 1½ in. (4 cm) from tip of nose, join ch to head with a ss (underneath).
- Make 14ch around nose to form noseband, join with a ss underneath.
- *Make 8ch at side of face and join to neckband just underneath ear.

Fasten off. Rep from * on other side of face.

Secure a red rose motif in place at side of headcollar.

pete the guinea pig

Pete is a close friend of Squiddly Dudley and they used to play together on the local football team. He wants to join Dudley in the Navy and sail around the world; he has had his medical and is waiting for the results. He used to have long hair but has cut it in anticipation.

body

- Using white, make 2ch.
- **Round 1:** 6sc in second ch from hook.
- **Round 2:** 2sc in each st. (12 sts)
- **Round 3:** *1sc in next st, 2sc in next st; rep from * to end. (18 sts)
- **Rounds 4–5:** 1sc in each st.
- **Round 6:** *1sc in next 2 sts, 2sc in next st; rep from * to end. (24 sts)
- **Rounds 7–11:** 1sc in each st.

Change to gold.

- **Rounds 12–16:** 1sc in each st.

Change to white.

- **Round 17:** 1sc in each st.
- **Round 18:** *1sc in next 2 sts, sc2tog; rep from * to end. (18 sts)
- **Rounds 19–20:** 1sc in each st.

Turn to right side. Insert safety eyes and secure. Stuff firmly.

Continue to work with wrong side facing.

- **Round 21:** *1sc in next st, sc2tog; rep from * to end.
- **Round 22:** Sc2tog until opening is closed.

Fasten off.

legs (make 4)

- Make 2ch.
- **Round 1:** 6sc in second ch from hook.
- **Rounds 2–4:** 1sc in each st.

Fasten off. Do not stuff.

Pin and sew to body at an angle facing the front.

ears (make 2)

- Make 2ch.
- **Round 1:** 6sc in second ch from hook.
- **Round 2:** 2sc in each st. (12 sts)
- **Round 3:** 1sc in each sc. (12 sts)

Fasten off. Pin and sew to head.

hair

Cut strands of yarn 2 in. (5 cm) long, knot into sts between ears to make tufts of hair. Trim.

face details

Cut a felt oval for nose. Sew to face.

Embroider mouth and nose details.

materials

Body, Legs, Ears: Rowan Pure Wool DK, shade 012 Snow (white)

Rowan Pure Wool DK, shade 033 Honey (gold)

Hair: Rowan Pure Wool DK, shade 016 Hessian (brown)

Nose: Pink felt and pink embroidery thread for detail

F/5 (4 mm) crochet hook

Pair safety eyes

Stuffing

abbreviations

ch chain; **sc** single crochet; **sc2tog** insert hook in st and draw up a loop. Insert hook in next st and draw up another loop. Yarn over, draw through all three loops on hook; **rep** repeat; **st(s)** stitch(es)

daisy the cow

Daisy is a hundred-mile-an-hour cow. She runs, dances, and moos loudly and loves to chase people in her field for fun. Once she chased two police officers and bit one on his leg; the other officer thought it was so funny he fell over in one of Daisy's cow pats. Have fun with the patches and make some random shapes.

materials

Head, Body, Legs: Rowan Pure Wool DK, shade 013 Enamel (cream)

Nostrils: Rowan Pure Wool DK, shade 025 Tea Rose (pink)

Horns: Rowan Pure Wool DK, shade 032 Gilt (yellow)

Hooves, Patches, Eyelashes: Rowan Pure Wool DK, shade 004 Black

Small Bell (do not use if toy is for small children)

Green gingham ribbon

F/5 (4 mm) & E/4 (3 mm) crochet hook

Pair of safety eyes

Stuffing

abbreviations

ch *chain;* **sc** *single crochet;* **sc2tog** *insert hook in st and draw up a loop. Insert hook in next st and draw up another loop. Yarn over, draw through all three loops on hook;* **rem** *remaining;* **rep** *repeat;* **ss** *slip stitch;* **st(s)** *stitch(es)*

head

- Using F/5 (4 mm) hook, make 2ch.
- **Round 1:** 6sc in second ch from hook.
- **Round 2:** 2sc in each st. (12 sts)
- **Round 3:** 2sc in each st to end. (24 sts)
- **Round 4:** *1sc in each of next 2 sts, sc2tog; rep from * to end. (18 sts)
- **Round 5:** *1sc in next 2 sts, 2sc in next st; rep from * to end. (24 sts)
- **Round 6:** *1sc in next 5 sts, 2sc in next st; rep from * to end. (28 sts)
- **Round 7:** *1sc in next 3 sts, 2sc in next st; rep from * to end. (35 sts)
- **Round 8:** *1sc in next 2 sts, sc2tog; rep from * to last 3 sts, 1sc in each st to end. (27 sts)
- **Round 9:** *1sc in next 2 sts, sc2tog; rep from * to last 3 sts, 1sc in each st to end. (21 sts)
- **Round 10:** *1sc in next st, sc2tog; rep from * to end. (14 sts)

Insert safety eyes and secure. Stuff head.

- **Round 11:** Sc2tog to end. (7 sts)
- **Round 12:** *Miss 1 st, 1sc in next st; rep from * to last st, ss in first sc.

Fasten off.

horns (make 2)

- Using D/3 (3 mm) hook make 2ch.
- **Round 1:** 6sc in second ch from hook.
- **Round 2:** 1sc in each st.
- **Round 3:** Sc2tog three times.
- **Round 4:** *Insert hook in next st and draw up a loop; rep from * twice, yarn over and draw through all four loops.

Fasten off. Do not stuff. Pin and sew to top of head.

ears (make 2)

- Using F/5 (4 mm) hook, make 6ch.
- **Round 1:** 1sc in second ch from hook, 1sc in each ch to last ch, 3sc in last ch.
- Working on other side of ch, 1sc in each st to end, ss in first sc.

Fasten off. Pin and sew to head.

body

- Using F/5 (4 mm) hook, make 2ch.
- **Round 1:** 6sc in second ch from hook.
- **Round 2:** 2sc in each st. (12 sts)
- **Round 3:** *1sc in next st, 2sc in next st; rep from * to end. (18 sts)
- **Round 4:** *1sc in next 2 sts, 2sc in next st; rep from * to end. (24 sts)
- **Round 5:** *1sc in next 3 sts, 2sc in next st; rep from * to end. (30 sts)
- **Round 6:** *1sc in next 4 sts, 2sc in next st; rep from * to end. (36 sts)
- **Rounds 7–14:** 1sc in each st.
- **Round 15:** *1sc in next 4 sts, sc2tog; rep from * to end. (30 sts)
- **Round 16:** *1sc in next 3 sts, sc2tog; rep from * to end. (24 sts)
- **Round 17:** *1sc in next 2 sts, sc2tog; rep from * to end. (18 sts)
- **Round 18:** 1sc in each st.

Stuff firmly.

- **Round 19:** *1sc in next st, sc2tog; rep from * to end. (12 sts)
- **Round 20:** *Miss 1 st, 1sc; rep from * to end. (6 sts)

Fasten off. Pin and sew to head.

legs (make 4)

- Using F/5 (4 mm) hook and black for hooves, make 2ch.
- **Round 1:** 8sc in second ch from hook.
- **Round 2:** 2sc in each st. (16 sts)
- **Round 3:** 1sc in each st.

Change to cream.

- **Round 4:** *1sc in each of next 2 sts, sc2tog; rep from * to end. (12 sts)
- **Round 5:** 1sc in each st until work measures 2¾ in. (7 cm).

Fasten off. Stuff firmly. Pin in position and sew to body.

patches

Using D/3 (3 mm) hook, make 5 patches or number as required.

small :

- Make 2ch.
- **Round 1:** 6sc in second ch from hook.
- **Round 2:** 2sc in each st. (12 sts)

Fasten off.

medium :

- Make 2ch
- **Round 1:** 6sc in second ch from hook.
- **Round 2:** 2sc in next 3 sts, 1sc in next 3 sts. (9 sts)
- **Round 3:** 2sc in next 3 sts, turn, 1sc in each st, ss in first sc.

Fasten off.

large :

- Make 2sc
- **Round 1:** 6sc in second ch from hook.
- **Round 2:** 2sc in next 2 sts, 1sc in next 2 sts, 2sc in next 2 sts. (10 sts)
- **Round 3:** 2sc in each st. (20 sts)
- **Round 4:** *1sc in next 2 sts, 2sc in next st; rep from * to last 2 sts, 1sc in last 2 sts. (26 sts).

Fasten off. Pin and sew patches on body and head.

tail

- Using F/5 (4 mm) hook and black, make 4ch. Change to cream, make 8ch.
- **Row 1:** Ss in second ch from hook, ss in each ch, use black for last 4 sts.

Fasten off. Sew cream end to body.

nostrils (make two)

- Using D/3 (3 mm) hook, make 2ch, 6sc in second ch from hook, ss in first sc.

Fasten off. Pin and sew in ends at the back and sew in place onto nose.

Embroider eyelashes. Thread small bell onto ribbon and tie round neck.

ned the naughty old goat

Ned used to live with the Buff-Orpingtons and for a while he thought he was a chicken. He now lives in the yard and if he gets the chance he loves eating through the Internet cable in the barn. He says it's the best thing he's ever tasted.

materials

Head, Body, Legs, Tail: Rooster Almerino DK, shade 202 Hazlenut (light brown)

Hooves, Mouth: Rowan Pure Wool DK, shade 004 (black)

Horns, Beard: Rooster Almerino DK, shade 201 Cornish (cream)

Eyes: White felt

Nostrils: Light brown felt

F/5 (4 mm) crochet hook

Pair of safety eyes

Stuffing

Sewing thread to match felt

abbreviations

ch *chain;* ***sc*** *single crochet;* ***sc2tog*** *insert hook in st and draw up a loop. Insert hook in next st and draw up another loop. Yarn over, draw through all three loops on hook;* ***hdc*** *half double;* ***rep*** *repeat;* ***ss*** *slip stitch;* ***st(s)*** *stitch(es)*

head

- Make 2ch.
- **Round 1:** 6sc in second ch from hook.
- **Round 2:** 2sc in each st. (12 sts)
- **Round 3:** *1sc in next 2 sts, 2sc in next st; rep from * to end. (16 sts)
- **Round 4:** *1sc in next 3 sts, 2sc in next st; rep from * to end. (20 sts)
- **Round 5:** *1sc in next 4 sts, 2sc in next st; rep from * to end. (24 sts)
- **Rounds 6–8:** 1sc in each st.
- **Round 9:** *1sc in next 2 sts, sc2tog; rep from * to end. (18 sts)
- **Round 10:** *1sc in next st, sc2tog; rep from * to end. (12 sts)

Cut small felt circles for backs of eyes. Make a small hole in the center and insert the safety eyes. Insert eyes in head and secure. Stuff head. Pin and sew felt pieces onto head.

- **Round 11:** Sc2tog to end. (6 sts)
- **Round 12:** *Miss 1 st, 1sc in next st; rep from * to end.

Fasten off.

horns (make 2)

- Make 2ch.
- **Round 1:** 6sc in second ch from hook.
- **Round 2:** 1sc in each st.
- **Round 3:** Sc2tog to end.
- **Round 4:** *Insert hook in next st and draw up a loop; rep from * twice more, yarn over and draw through all 4 loops on the hook.

Fasten off. Do not stuff. Pin and sew to top of head.

ears (make 2)

- Make 6ch.
- 1sc in second ch from hook, 1sc in next 3 ch, 3sc in last ch, working in other side of ch, 1sc in each ch to end, ss in first sc.

Fasten off. Pin and sew to head.

body

- Make 2ch.
- **Round 1:** 6sc in second ch from hook.
- **Round 2:** 2sc in each st. (12 sts)
- **Round 3:** *1sc in next st, 2sc in next st; rep from * to end. (18 sts)
- **Round 4:** *1sc in next 2 sts, 2sc in next st; rep from * to end. (24 sts)
- **Round 5:** *1sc in next 3 sts, 2sc in next st; rep from * to end. (30 sts)
- **Round 6:** *1sc in next 4 sts, 2sc in next st; rep from * to end. (36 sts)
- **Rounds 7–14:** 1sc in each st.
- **Round 15:** *1sc in next 4 sts, sc2tog; rep from * to end. (30 sts)
- **Round 16:** *1sc in next 3 sts, sc2tog; rep from * to end. (24 sts)
- **Round 17:** *1sc in next 2 sts, sc2tog; rep from * to end. (18 sts)
- **Round 18:** 1sc in each st.

Stuff body firmly.

- **Round 19:** *1sc in next st, sc2tog; rep from * to end. (12 sts)
- **Round 20:** *Miss 1st, 1sc in next st; rep from * to end. (6 sts)

Fasten off. Pin and sew to head.

legs (make 4)

- Using black, make 2ch.
- **Round 1:** 6sc in second ch from hook.
- **Round 2:** 2sc in each st. (12 sts)
- **Round 3:** 1sc in each st.

Change to light brown:

- **Round 4:** *1sc in next 2 sts, sc2tog; rep from * to end. (9 sts)
- **Round 5:** 1sc in each st until work measures approx 3⅛ in. (8 cm).

Fasten off. Stuff firmly.

Pin and sew to body.

tail

- 7ch, 2hdc in second ch from hook, 1sc in each ch to end. Fasten off. Pin and sew to body.

face details

Cut 2 small ovals of felt for nostrils. Pin and sew in place.

Embroider mouth. Cut 8–10 strands of cream for beard and knot through stitches underneath chin. Trim.

the two little pigs

Tiggy and Mitzi live in the countryside. They are vegetarian and keen animal rights activists. Recently they have started a protest group PETA—Pigs for the Ethical Treatment of Animals—and have organized a fundraising barn dance. One friend suggested they put on a hog roast. They weren't amused!

head

- Make 2ch.
- **Round 1:** 6sc in second ch from hook.
- **Round 2:** 2sc in each st. (12 sts)
- **Round 3:** *1sc in next st, 2sc in next st; rep from * to end. (18 sts)
- **Round 4:** *1sc in next 2 sts, 2sc in next st; rep from * to end. (24 sts)
- **Round 5:** *1sc in next 3 sts, 2sc in next st; rep from * to end. (30 sts)
- **Round 6:** *1sc in next 4 sts, 2sc in next st; rep from * to end. (36 sts)
- **Round 7:** 1sc in each st.
- **Round 8:** *1sc in next 4 sts, sc2tog; rep from * to end. (30 sts)
- **Round 9:** *1sc in next 3 sts, sc2tog; rep from * to end. (24 sts)
- **Round 10:** *1sc in next 2 sts, sc2tog; rep from * to end. (18 sts)
- **Round 11:** 1sc in each st.
- **Round 12:** *1sc in next st, sc2tog; rep from * to end. (12 sts)

Insert eyes in face and secure. Stuff firmly.

- **Round 13:** *Miss 1 st, 1sc in next st; rep from * until opening is closed.

Fasten off.

body

- Make 2ch.
- **Round 1:** 6sc in second ch from hook.
- **Round 2:** 2sc in each st. (12 sts)
- **Round 3:** *1sc in next st, 2sc in next st; rep from * to end. (18 sts)
- **Rounds 4–10:** 1sc in each st.
- **Round 11:** Sc2tog to end. (9 sts)

Fasten off. Stiff firmly.

Pin and sew to head.

arms (make 2)

- Make 2ch.
- **Round 1:** 6sc in second ch from hook.
- **Round 2:** 1sc in each st.

Continue until arms measure 1½ in. (4 cm).

Fasten off. Do not stuff.

Pin and sew to body.

legs (make 2)

- Make 2ch.
- **Round 1:** 6sc in second ch from hook.
- **Round 2:** 1sc in each st.

Continue until legs measure 1½ in. (4 cm).

Fasten off. Do not stuff.

Pin and sew to body.

ears (make 2)

- Make 7ch.
- **Row 1:** 1sc in second ch from hook, 1sc in each ch. (6 sts)
- **Row 2:** 1sc in each st.
- **Row 3:** Sc2tog, 1sc in next 2 sts, sc2tog. (4 sts)
- **Row 4:** 1sc in each st.
- **Row 5:** Sc2tog, twice. (2 sts)
- **Row 6:** Sc2tog.

Fasten off.

Pin and sew to head.

face detail

Cut a round felt muzzle and sew on to face. Cut two small felt ovals and sew on to muzzle.

Embroider mouth.

dress

Using dress template, cut from a folded piece of fabric or felt with the fold at the top of the shoulders. If making with fabric, pin and sew the hems if possible. There is no need to hem if making with felt. Turn right side out and press seams. Place very carefully on piggy, placing the legs through the neck of the dress and gently easing upward onto body. (Head is big for neck opening, so if putting over head, place very carefully making sure not to stretch neck space.)

Sew rose motif onto front of dress.

materials

Head, Body, Arms, Legs: Rooster Almerino DK, Strawberry Cream (light pink)

Muzzle: Dark pink felt

Nose: Light pink felt

Mouth: Black embroidery thread

Dress 1: Red gingham cotton, pink rose motif

Dress 2: Blue felt, red rose motif

F/5 (4 mm) crochet hook

Pair safety eyes

Stuffing

Sewing thread to match felt

abbreviations

ch *chain;* ***sc*** *single crochet;* ***sc2tog*** *insert hook in st and draw up a loop. Insert hook in next st and draw up another loop. Yarn over, draw through all three loops on hook;* ***rep*** *repeat;* ***ss*** *slip stitch;* ***st(s)*** *stitch(es)*

pickle the puppy

Pickle wears his scarf so that he doesn't just look like any other dog on the street. Pickle is not ordinary, he loves to perform tricks and can do somersaults, play football, basketball, and hockey. His dream is to be in the next Olympics and he is also an excellent diver. He works up a big appetite from being so energetic and loves eating pasta, especially tagliatelle. He uses his scarf as a napkin when he's eating and has several in a range of bright colors.

head

- Make 2ch.
- **Round 1:** 6sc in second ch from hook.
- **Round 2:** 2sc in each st. (12 sts)
- **Round 3:** *1sc in next 2 sts, 2sc in next st; rep from * to end. (16 sts)
- **Round 4:** *1sc in next 3 sts, 2sc in next st; rep from * to end. (20 sts)
- **Round 5:** *1sc in next 4 sts, 2sc in next st; rep from * to end. (24 sts)
- **Rounds 6–8:** 1sc in each st.
- **Round 9:** *1sc in next 2 sts, sc2tog; rep from * to end. (18 sts)
- **Round 10:** *1sc in next st, sc2tog; rep from * to end. (12 sts)

Insert eyes and secure. Stuff head.

- **Round 11:** *Sc2tog; rep from * until opening is closed.

Fasten off.

muzzle

- Make 2ch.
- **Round 1:** 6sc in second ch from hook.
- **Round 2:** 2sc in each st. (12 sts)
- **Rounds 3–4:** 1sc in each st.

Fasten off. Stuff muzzle lightly.

Pin and sew to face. Embroider nose and mouth details.

ears (make 2)

- Make 2ch.
- **Round 1:** 6sc in second ch from hook.
- **Round 2:** 1sc in each st.
- **Round 3:** 2sc in each st. (12 sts)
- **Rounds 4–5:** 1sc in each st.
- **Round 6:** *Sc2tog, 1sc in next 4 sts; rep from * once. (10 sts)

Fasten off.

Work running stitch around inside edge of ears, up three sides only, leaving base open. This defines the shape of the ears. Gently push finger up through opening to open the ears and shape. Pin and sew to head.

body

- Make 2ch.
- **Round 1:** 6sc in second chain from hook.
- **Round 2:** 2sc in each st. (12 sts)
- **Round 3:** *1sc in next st, 2sc in next st; rep from * to

end. (18 sts)
- **Round 4:** *1sc in next 2 sts, 2sc in next st; rep from * to end. (24 sts)
- **Round 5:** *1sc in next 3 sts, 2sc in next st; rep from * to end. (30 sts)
- **Rounds 6–15:** 1sc in each st.
- **Round 16:** *1sc in next 3 sts, sc2tog; rep from * to end. (24 sts)
- **Round 17:** *1sc in next 2 sts, sc2tog; rep from * to end. (18 sts)

Stuff firmly.

- **Round 18:** *1sc in next st, sc2tog; rep from * to end. (12 sts)
- **Round 19:** *Miss 1 st, 1sc in next st; rep from * until opening is closed.

Fasten off, sew in ends. Pin and sew to head.

legs (make 4)

- Make 2ch.
- **Round 1:** 5sc in second ch from hook.
- **Round 2:** 2sc in each st. (10 sts)
- **Round 3:** 1sc in each st.
- **Round 4:** *1sc in each of next 3 sts, sc2tog; rep from * once. (8 sts)
- **Round 4:** 1sc in each st until work measures 2¾ in. (7cm).

Fasten off. Stuff. Pin in position and sew to body.

tail

- Make 2ch.
- **Round 1:** 4sc in second ch from hook.
- **Round 2:** 2sc in next st, 1sc in each st to last st, 2sc in last st. (6 sts)
- **Round 3:** *1sc in next st, 2sc in next st; rep from * to end. (9 sts)
- **Rounds 4–6:** 1sc in each st.
- **Round 7:** *Sc2tog, 1sc in next st; rep from * to end. (6 sts)
- **Rounds 8–9:** 1sc in each st.

Fasten off. Stuff lightly. Pin and sew to body.

scarf

Use template to cut out scarf. Hem edges. Tie around Pickle's neck.

materials

Head, Body, Legs, Tail: Debbie Bliss, Cotton DK shade 35 (yellow)

Nose: Debbie Bliss, Rialto DK shade 03 (black)

Mouth: Debbie Bliss, Rialto DK shade 13 (pink)

Scarf: Small piece of fabric

F/5 (4 mm) crochet hook

Pair of safety eyes

Stuffing

abbreviations

ch *chain;* ***sc*** *single crochet;* ***sc2tog*** *insert hook in st and draw up a loop. Insert hook in next st and draw up another loop. Yarn over, draw through all three loops on hook;* ***rep*** *repeat;* ***ss*** *slip stitch;* ***st(s)*** *stitch(es)*

melody the kitten

Melody would like to be a ballerina and practices in her room for at least an hour a day. She loves the color pink and always makes sure she's wearing a pink item of clothing. She's in love with Alan the Lion, and when she grows up she would like to join his ska band as the lead singer.

head

- Make 2ch.
- **Round 1:** 6sc in second ch from hook.
- **Round 2:** 2sc in each st. (12 sts)
- **Round 3:** *1sc in next st. 2sc in next st; rep from * to end. (18 sts)
- **Round 4:** *1sc in next 2 sts. 2sc in next st; rep from * to end. (24 sts)
- **Round 5:** *1sc in next 3 sts, 2sc in next st; rep from * to end. (30 sts)
- **Round 6:** *1sc in next 4 sts, 2sc in next st; rep from * to end. (36 sts)
- **Round 7:** 1sc in each st.
- **Round 8:** *1sc in next 4 sts, sc2tog; rep from * to end. (30 sts)
- **Round 9:** *1sc in next 3 sts, sc2tog; rep from * to end. (24 sts)
- **Round 10:** *1sc in next 2 sts, sc2tog; rep from * to end. (18 sts)
- **Round 11:** 1sc in each st.
- **Round 12:** *1sc in next st, sc2tog; rep from * to end. (12 sts)

Insert eyes in head and secure. Stuff firmly.

- **Round 13:** *Miss 1 st, 1sc in next st; rep from * until opening is closed.

Fasten off.

body

- Make 2ch.
- **Round 1:** 6sc in second ch from hook.
- **Round 2:** 2sc in each st. (12 sts)
- **Round 3:** *1sc in next st, 2sc in next st; rep from * to end. (18 sts)
- **Rounds 4–9:** 1sc in each st.
- **Round 10:** *1sc in next st, sc2tog; rep from * to end. (12 sts)

Fasten off. Stuff.

Pin and sew to head.

arms (make 2)

- Make 2ch.
- **Round 1:** 6sc in second ch from hook.
- **Round 2:** 1sc in each st.

Continue until arms measure 1½ in. (4 cm).

Fasten off. Do not stuff.

Pin and sew to body.

legs (make 2)

- Make 2ch.
- **Round 1:** 6sc in second ch from hook.
- **Round 2:** 1sc in each st.
- Continue until legs measure 1½ in. (4 cm).

Fasten off. Do not stuff.

Pin and sew to body.

ears (make 2)

- Make 5 ch
- **Row 1:** 1sc in second ch from hook, 1sc in each ch.
- **Row 2:** 1ch, 1sc in each sc.

Rep Row 2 until work forms a square.

Fold square in half to make a triangle and sc sides together, at top point make 2sc.

Fasten off.

Pin and sew to head.

face detail

Embroider a flower below ear.

Cut out a felt oval for muzzle. Cut out a felt triangle for nose and sew to muzzle. Sew muzzle to head.

Embroider mouth detail and whiskers.

dress

- Make 50ch.

frill

Ss in second ch from hook, *miss 1ch, 3dc in next ch, miss 1ch, ss in next ch; rep from * to end.

Then work into other side of ch, so frill edge is facing downward.

- **Next row:** 3ch, *1dc in same ch as 3dc, 1dc in same ch as ss; rep from * to end. (25 sts)
- **Next row:** 1ch, 1sc in each st, 1ch, turn.

Rep last row twice.

- **Next row:** Miss 1 st, 1sc in each st to end, 1ch, turn.
- **Next row:** Miss 1 st, 1sc in each st to end.

Fasten off. Join center back seam.

dress straps

The following is a guide to where to place the straps. Depending on your tension this could vary. Fit dress onto kitten and mark with pins where straps should be worked.

- *Join yarn at one front marker, 7ch, ss in corresponding back marker, 1ch, 1sc in each ch, ss in same place as join.

Fasten off.

Work second strap as first.

Fit dress on kitten.

bubbles the rabbit

Bubbles is one of a kind in a field of many. Her friends are all the other animals; she looks after the mice and is best friends with Tiggy and Mitzi the little pigs. She really likes carrot cake but not stew. Next year she will be working as an air hostess for British Hareways flying between London and New York.

head

- Make 2ch.
- **Round 1:** 6sc in second ch from hook.
- **Round 2:** 2sc in each st. (12 sts)
- **Round 3:** *1sc in next st, 2sc in next st; rep from * to end. (18 sts)
- **Round 4:** *1sc in next 2 sts, 2sc in next st; rep from * to end. (24 sts)
- **Round 5:** *1sc in next 3 sts, 2sc in next st; rep from * to end. (30 sts)
- **Round 6:** *1sc in next 4 sts, 2sc in next st; rep from * to end. (36 sts)
- **Round 7:** 1sc in each st.
- **Round 8:** *1sc in next 4 sts, sc2tog; rep from * to end. (30 sts)
- **Round 9:** *1sc in next 3 sts, sc2tog; rep from * to end. (24 sts)
- **Round 10:** *1sc in next 2 sts, sc2tog; rep from * to end. (18 sts)
- **Round 11:** 1sc in each st.
- **Round 12:** *1sc in next st, sc2tog; rep from * to end. (12 sts)

Insert eyes in place and secure. Stuff head firmly.

- **Round 13:** *Miss 1st, 1sc in next st; rep from * until opening is closed.

Fasten off.

body

- Make 2ch.
- **Round 1:** 6sc in second ch from hook.
- **Round 2:** 2sc in each st. (12 sts)
- **Round 3:** *1sc in next st, 2sc in next st; rep from * to end. (18 sts)
- **Rounds 4–10:** 1sc in each st.

Fasten off.

Stuff. Pin and sew to head.

arms

- Make 2ch.
- **Round 1:** 6sc in second ch from hook.
- **Round 2:** 1sc in each st.

Continue until arms measure 1¼ in. (3 cm).

Fasten off. Do not stuff. Pin and sew to body.

legs

- Make 2ch.
- **Round 1:** 6sc in second ch from hook.
- **Round 2:** 1sc in each st.
- Continue until legs measure 1¼ in. (3 cm).

Fasten off. Do not stuff. Pin and sew to body.

ears

- Make 2ch.
- **Round 1:** 6sc in second ch from hook.
- **Rounds 2–6:** 1sc in each st.

Fasten off. Do not stuff. Pin and sew to head.

tail

- Make a small pom pom and sew on body.

face detail

Cut out a felt oval for muzzle and a felt triangle for nose. Sew nose on muzzle. Embroider mouth detail and sew muzzle to head.

Make a small bow and sew to center of head.

materials

Head, Body, Arms, Legs: Rooster Almerino DK, 205 Glace (light blue)

Tail: Rowan Pure Wool DK, 012 Snow (white)

Muzzle: Light pink felt

Nose: Black felt

Mouth: Black embroidery thread

Bow: Pink gingham ribbon

F/5 (4 mm) crochet hook

Pair safety eyes

Stuffing

abbreviations

ch *chain;* **sc** *single crochet;* **sc2tog** *insert hook in st and draw up a loop. Insert hook in next st and draw up another loop. Yarn over, draw through all three loops on hook;* **rem** *remaining;* **rep** *repeat;* **ss** *slip stitch;* **st(s)** *stitch(es)*

sugar mice

Maddy, Lily, and Lydia are giggly and loud mice. They love going to parties, shopping, and flying away on holiday together. Last year Lydia and Maddy took their boat to Cape Cod and drove in the middle of the harbour; it broke down and the Fish Brothers had to rescue them. They quite enjoyed it. They are called the Sugar Mice because they can't stop eating candy.

materials

Mouse 1: RYC Cashsoft DK, shade 501 Sweet (pink)

Mouse 2: RYC Cashsoft DK, shade 509 Lime (green)

Mouse 3: Rowan Pure Wool DK, shade 032 Gilt (yellow)

Nose: White felt

Whiskers: White embroidery thread

F/5 (4 mm) crochet hook

Pair safety eyes

Stuffing

abbreviations

ch chain; sc single crochet; sc2tog insert hook in st and draw up a loop. Insert hook in next st and draw up another loop. Yarn over, draw through all three loops on hook; rep repeat; ss slip stitch; st(s) stitch(es)

body

- Make 2ch.
- **Round 1:** 6sc in second ch from hook.
- **Round 2:** 2sc in each st. (12 sts).
- **Round 3:** *1sc in next st, 2sc in next st; rep from * to end. (18 sts)
- **Round 4:** *1sc in next 2 sts, 2sc in next st; rep from * to end. (24 sts)
- **Round 5:** *1sc in next 3 sts, 2sc in next st; rep from * to end. (30 sts)
- **Round 6:** *1sc in next 4 sts, 2sc in next st; rep from * to end. (36 sts)
- **Rounds 7–14:** 1sc in each st.
- **Round 15:** *1sc in next 4 sts, sc2tog; rep from * to end. (30 sts)
- **Round 16:** *1sc in next 3 sts, sc2tog; rep from * to end. (24 sts)
- **Round 17:** 1sc in each st.
- **Round 18:** *1sc in next 2 sts, sc2tog; rep from * to end. (18 sts)
- **Round 19:** 1sc in each st.
- **Round 20:** *1sc in next st, sc2tog; rep from * to end. (12 sts).

Insert eyes and secure. Stuff body.

- **Rounds 21–22:** 1sc in each st.
- **Round 23** *Miss 1 st, 1sc in next st; rep from * until opening is closed.

Fasten off.

ears (make 2)

- Make 2ch.
- **Round 1:** 6sc in second st from hook.
- **Round 2:** 2sc in each st. (12 sts)
- **Round 3:** 1sc in each st.

Fasten off. Sew behind eyes.

tail

- Make 20ch, turn, ss in each ch.

Fasten off.

Pin and sew to body.

dimitri the donkey

Dimitri is originally from Greece. He is a seaside donkey and lives by the ocean near Daytona Beach. He came over to Florida from Greece because he fell in love with one of the Sugar Mice, Lily. She taught him all the English he knows, but he's still learning. He talks to all the old ladies on the beach, but sometimes they can't understand him and when he says "*efcareesto,*" which means "thank you," they think he's saying "a ferret's toe."

materials

Head, Neck, Ears, Body, Legs, Neck, Tail: Rowan Pure Wool DK, shade 018 Earth (brown)

Muzzle, Tail, Hooves: Rowan Pure Wool DK, shade 012 Snow (white)

Hat: Rowan Pure Wool DK, shade 032 Gilt (yellow)

Eyes: White felt

F/5 (4 mm) crochet hook

Pair safety eyes

Stuffing

Sewing thread to match felt

abbreviations

ch *chain;* **sc** *single crochet;* **sc2tog** *insert hook in st and draw up a loop. Insert hook in next st and draw up another loop. Yarn over, draw through all three loops on hook;* **rep** *repeat;* **ss** *slip stitch;* **st(s)** *stitch(es)*

head

- Using white yarn for muzzle, make 2ch.
- **Round 1:** 6sc in second ch from hook.
- **Round 2:** 2sc in each st. (12 sts)
- **Rounds 3–4:** 1sc in each st.

Change to brown.

- **Rounds 5–7:** 1sc in each st.
- **Round 8:** 1sc in each of next 3 sts, make 2sc in each of the next 6 sts, 1sc in each of last 3 sts. (18 sts)
- **Round 9:** *1sc in each of next 2 sts, 2sc in next st; rep from * to end. (24 sts)
- **Rounds 10–14:** 1sc in each st.

Cut two small white felt circles, make a small hole in the center, insert safety eyes, push in face, and secure. Stuff head. Sew felt to head.

- **Round 15:** *1sc in next st, sc2tog; rep from * to end. (12 sts)
- **Round 17:** Sc2tog; rep from * to end.

Fasten off.

neck

- Make 16ch, ss in first ch to form a ring.
- **Round 1:** 1sc in each ch to end.
- **Rounds 2–6:** 1sc in each st.
- **Rounds 7–8:** Ss in first 8 sts, 1sc in last 8 sts.

Fasten off. Stuff.

Pin and sew to back of head.

ears (make 2)

- Make 2ch.
- **Round 1:** 6sc in second ch from hook.
- **Round 2:** *1sc in next st, 2sc in next st; rep from * to end. (9 sts)
- **Rounds 3–8:** 1sc in each st.
- **Round 9:** *1sc in next st, sc2tog; rep from * to end. (6 sts)
- **Round 10:** Sc2tog to end.

Fasten off.

Flatten ears, leaving base open. Work a running stitch around edge of ears, leaving base open. This defines the shape of the ears. Gently push finger up through opening to open the ears and shape. These will be sewn on later.

body

- Make 2ch.
- **Round 1:** 6sc in second ch from hook.
- **Round 2:** 2sc in each st. (12 sts)
- **Round 3:** *1sc in next st, 2sc in next st; rep from * to end. (18 sts)
- **Round 4:** *1sc in next 2 sts, 2sc in next st; rep from * to end. (24 sts)
- **Round 5:** *1sc in next 3 sts, 2sc in next st; rep from * to end. (30 sts)
- **Round 6:** *1sc in next 4 sts, 2sc in next st; rep from * to end. (36 sts)
- **Rounds 7–14:** 1sc in each st.
- **Round 15:** *1sc in next 4 sts, sc2tog; rep from * to end. (30 sts)

- **Round 16:** *1sc in next 3 sts, sc2tog; rep from * to end. (24 sts)
- **Round 17:** *1sc in next 2 sts, sc2tog; rep from * to end. (18 sts)
- **Round 18:** Make 1sc in each st.

Stuff firmly.

- **Round 19:** *1sc in next st, sc2tog; rep from * to end.
- **Round 20:** Miss 1 st, 1sc; rep from * to end. (6 sts)

Fasten off. Pin and sew to head.

legs (make 4)

- Using white yarn, make 2ch for hoof.
- **Round 1:** 5sc in second ch from hook.
- **Round 2:** 2sc in each st. (10 sts)
- **Round 3:** 1sc in each st.
- **Round 4:** *1sc in each of next 3 sts, sc2tog; rep from * to end. (8 sts)

Change to brown.

- **Round 5:** 1sc in each st until work measures 2¾ in. (7 cm).

Fasten off. Stuff. Pin and sew to body.

tail

- Using white make 3ch, change to brown, make 13ch.
- **Row 1:** Ss in second ch from hook, ss in each ch, changing to white for last 3 sts.

Fasten off. Sew to body.

straw hat

- Make 2ch.
- **Round 1:** 6sc in second ch from hook.
- **Round 2:** 2sc in each st. (12 sts)
- **Round 3:** 1sc in each st.
- **Round 4:** *1sc in next st, 2sc in next st; rep from * to end. (18 sts)
- **Round 5:** *3ch, *miss 3 sts, 1sc in next 6 sts; rep from * to end. (18 sts)
- **Round 6:** *1sc in each of next 3ch, 1sc in each of next 6 sts; rep from * to end. (18 sts)
- **Round 7:** 2sc in each st. (36 sts)
- **Round 8:** 1sc in each st.

Fasten off.

Cut 36 strands 2 in. (4 cm) long. Using one strand at a time, knot through each st around edge of hat, pulling the two ends of the strand through the loop to secure. When all tassels are made, trim.

Pin and sew ears to head after you have made hat. Pin hat and ears at the same time to ensure you have ears in the correct position.

Place hat on head pushing ears through holes made. Push a small amount of stuffing in inside top of hat and secure hat by making small stitches through hat to head.

cheryl the snail

materials

Head, Body, Tail: Rooster Almerino DK, shade 207 Gooseberry (green)

Shell: Rooster Almerino DK, shade 203 Strawberry Cream (light pink)

Antennae: Rowan Pure Wool DK, shade 032 Gilt (yellow)

F/5 (4 mm) crochet hook

Pair safety eyes

Stuffing

abbreviations

ch chain; sc single crochet; sc2tog insert hook in st and draw up a loop. Insert hook in next st and draw up another loop. Yarn over, draw through all three loops on hook; hdc(s) half double(s); rep repeat; ss slip stitch; st(s) stitch(es)

Cheryl is a marvelous cook; she cooks all the vegetables and salad that grow in the garden to make delicious recipes for her friends. She avoids the lettuce beds when she's collecting her ingredients at night because the slugs are often having a rowdy party in the beer left out for them in the garden.

head, body, and tail (make all as one)

Begin at tail end.

- Make 2ch.
- **Row 1:** 1sc in second ch from hook.
- **Row 2:** 1ch, 2sc in next st.
- **Row 3:** 1ch, 2sc in each st. (4 sts)
- **Row 4:** 1ch, 2sc in first st, 1sc in next 2 sts, 2sc in last st. (6 sts)
- **Row 5:** 1ch, 1sc in next 2 sts, 2sc in next st, 1sc in next 3 sts. (7 sts)
- **Round 1:** 2sc in each st. (14 sts)
- **Rounds 2–9:** 1sc in each st. (14 sts)
- **Rounds 10–11:** 1sc in next 4 sts, ss in next 6 sts, 1sc in next 4 sts.
- **Rounds 12–21:** 1sc in each st. (14 sts)

Insert eyes and secure. Stuff, keeping tail flat and body in the upright position.

- **Round 22:** 1sc in each of next 2 sts, sc2tog, 1sc in each of next 2 sts, sc2tog, 1sc in each of next 2 sts, sc2tog, 1sc in each of last 2 sts. (11 sts)
- **Round 23:** 1sc in each of next 2 sts, sc2tog, 1sc in each of next 2 sts, sc2tog, 1sc in each of last 3 sts. (9 sts)
- **Round 24:** Sc2tog, 4 times, 1sc in last sc. (5 sts)

Fasten off.

shell

- Make 2ch.
- **Round 1:** 6sc in second ch from hook.
- **Round 2:** 2sc in each st. (12 sts)
- **Round 3:** *1sc in next st, 2sc in next st; rep from * to end. (18 sts)
- **Round 4:** *1sc in next 2 sts, 2sc in next st; rep from * to end. (24 sts)
- **Round 5:** *1sc in next 3 sts, 2sc in next st; rep from * to end. (30 sts)
- **Rounds 6–8:** 1sc in each st.
- **Round 9:** 1sc in next 3 sts, sc2tog; rep from * to end. (24 sts)
- **Round 10:** *1sc in next 2 sts, sc2tog; rep from * to end. (18 sts)
- **Round 11:** 1sc in each st.

Stuff firmly.

- **Round 12:** *1sc in next st, sc2tog; rep from * to end. (12 sts)
- **Round 13:** Sc2tog to end. (12 sts)
- **Round 14:** Miss 1 st, 1sc in next st; rep from * to end.

Fasten off.

Pin and sew to body.

antennae (make 2)

- Make 7ch, 2hdc in second ch from hook, ss in each ch to end.

Fasten off.

Pin and sew to head.

exotic animals

Squiddly Dudley is making a big pot of chili and everyone is invited. Buzz the Emu is bringing Alphonso the Alpaca and the Fish Brothers in the DeLorean. Dave the Dolphin and Freddie the Seal are riding the bus, and Vince the Rhinestone Spider is bringing his piano so he can do his Neil Diamond impressions.

Buzz

Oscar

Alan

Shakira

alan the lion

materials

Head, Body, Ears, Tail, Arms, Legs: Rooster Almerino DK, shade 202 Hazlenut (light brown)

Hair: Rooster Almerino DK, shade 210 Custard (yellow)

Muzzle: Beige felt

Nose: Light brown felt

Mouth: Black embroidery thread

F/5 (4 mm) crochet hook

Pair safety eyes

Stuffing

Sewing thread to match felt

abbreviations

ch *chain;* **rep** *repeat;* **sc** *single crochet;* **sc2tog** *insert hook in st and draw up a loop. Insert hook in next st and draw up another loop. Yarn over, draw through all three loops on hook;* **st(s)** *stitch(es)*

Alan plays the saxophone in a ska band. He sometimes wears a pork pie hat but it keeps falling off because of his mane. He plays indie and rock music on his ipod and likes retro music; he also taps his foot to "The Lion Sleeps Tonight."

head

- Make 2ch.
- **Round 1:** 6sc in second ch from hook.
- **Round 2:** 2sc in each st. (12 sts)
- **Round 3:** *1sc in next st, 2sc in next st; rep from * to end. (18 sts)
- **Round 4:** *1sc in next 2 sts. 2sc in next st; rep from * to end. (24 sts)
- **Round 5:** *1sc in next 3 sts. 2sc in next st; rep from * to end. (30 sts)
- **Round 6:** *1sc in next 4 sts. 2sc in next st; rep from * to end. (36 sts)
- **Round 7:** 1sc in each st.
- **Round 8:** *1sc in next 4 sts, sc2tog; rep from * to end. (30 sts)
- **Round 9:** *1sc in next 3 sts, sc2tog; rep from * to end. (24 sts)
- **Round 10:** *1sc in next 2 sts, sc2tog; rep from * to end. (18 sts)
- **Round 11:** 1sc in each st.
- **Round 12:** *1sc in next st, sc2tog; rep from * to end. (12 sts)

Insert eyes and secure. Stuff head firmly.

- **Round 13:** *Miss 1 st, 1sc in next st; rep from * until opening is closed.

Fasten off.

body

- Make 2ch.
- **Round 1:** 6sc in second ch from hook.
- **Round 2:** 2sc in each st. (12 sts)
- **Round 3:** *1sc in next st, 2sc in next st; rep from * to end. (18 sts)
- **Rounds 4–10:** 1sc in each st.

Fasten off. Stuff and sew to head.

arms

- Make 2ch.
- **Round 1:** 6sc in second ch from hook.
- **Round 2:** 1sc in each st.

Continue until arms measure 1½ in. (4 cm).

Fasten off. Do not stuff. Pin and sew to body.

legs

- Make 2ch.
- **Round 1:** 6sc in second ch from hook.
- **Round 2:** 1sc in each st.

Continue until legs measure 2 in. (5 cm).

Fasten off. Do not stuff. Pin and sew to body.

ears

- Make 2ch.
- **Round 1:** 6sc in second ch from hook.
- **Round 2:** 2sc in each st to end. (12 sts)
- **Round 3:** 1sc in each st.

Fasten off. Pin and sew to head.

face details

Cut a felt oval for muzzle. Cut a small felt triangle for nose and sew on muzzle. Embroider mouth with black embroidery thread. Pin and sew onto center of Lion's face.

tail

- Using yellow, make 2ch.
- **Round 1:** 6sc in second ch from hook.
- **Rounds 2–3:** 1sc in each st.

Change to light brown.

- 1sc in each st until tail measures 2½ in. (6.5 cm).

Fasten off.

Using yellow, make a small tassle and attach to end of tail. Pin and sew to body.

mane

Using yellow yarn cut lots of 4 in. (10 cm) strands. Thread through two strands together at the same time round face, neck and around back of head. Trim ends to shape.

elliot & shakira the baby elephants

Elliot and Shakira are best friends. They are being brought up in a very ethical circus where all the animals are really well looked after. Elliot loves to play video games all day at the local arcade. Shakira likes nothing better than watching her mother, who is one of the stars of the circus, practice her special trapeze act where she swings around very high up in the tent by her trunk.

trunk

Note: Trunk, head, neck and body are made as one and worked with wrong side facing.
- Make 2ch.
- **Round 1:** 6sc in second ch from hook.
- **Round 2:** 1sc in each st.

Continue until trunk measures 2 ¼in. (6 cm). Do not fasten off.

head

- **Round 1:** *2sc in next st, 1 sc in next st; rep from * to end. (9 sts)
- **Round 2:** *2sc in next st, 1sc in next st; rep from * to last st, 1sc in last st. (13 sts)
- **Round 3:** *1sc in each of next 2 sts, 2sc in next st; rep from * to last st, 1sc in last st. (17 sts)
- **Round 4:** *1sc in each of next 3 sts, 2sc in next st; rep from * until last st, 1sc in last st. (21 sts)
- **Round 5:** *1sc in each of next 4 sts, 2sc in next st; rep from * to last st, 1sc in last st. (25 sts)
- **Rounds 6–8:** 1sc in each st.
- **Round 9:** *1sc in each of next 4 sts, sc2tog; rep from * to last st, 1sc in last st. (21 sts)
- **Round 10:** *1sc in each of next 3 sts, sc2tog; rep from * to last st, 1sc in last st. (17 sts)
- **Round 11:** *1sc in each of next 2 sts, sc2tog; rep from * to last st, 1sc in last st. (13 sts)

Insert safety eyes and secure. Stuff. Do not fasten off.

neck and body

- **Round 12:** 2sc in each st. (26 sts)
- **Rounds 13–14:** 1sc in each st.
- **Round 15:** *1sc in each of next 4 sts, 2sc in next st; rep from * to last st, 1sc in last st. (31 sts)
- **Rounds 16–21:** 1sc in each st.
- **Round 22:** *1sc in next 4 sts, 2sc tog; rep from * to last st, 1sc in last st. (26 sts)
- **Round 23:** *1sc in next 3 sts, 2sc tog; rep from * to last st, 1sc in last st. (21 sts)
- **Round 24:** *1sc in next 2 sts, 2sc tog; rep from * to last st, 1sc in last st. (16 sts)
- **Round 25:** 1sc in each st.

Stuff neck and body.

- **Round 26:** *Miss 1 st, 1sc in next st; rep from * until opening is closed.

Fasten off.

ears (make 2)

- Make 11ch.
- **Row 1:** 2sc in next st from hook, 1sc in next 8 ch, 2sc in last st, turn. (12 sts)
- **Row 2:** 1sc in each st.
- **Row 3:** Sc2tog, 1sc in next 8 sts, sc2tog in last 2 sts. (10 sts)
- **Row 4:** Sc2tog, 1sc in next 6 sts, sc2tog in last 2 sts. (8 sts)
- **Rows 5–6:** 1sc in each st.
- **Row 7:** Sc2tog, 1sc in next 4 sts, sc2tog. (6 sts)

Fasten off.

Pin and sew ears in place.

materials

Trunk, Head, Body, Ears, Tail: RYC Cashsoft DK, shade 505 (gray)

Legs: (Girl) RYC Cashsoft DK, shade 501 Sweet (pink), Cashsoft DK, shade 505 (gray). (Boy) RYC Cashsoft DK, shade 509 Lime (green), Cashsoft DK, shade 505 (gray)

Tail Tassel: RYC Cashsoft DK, shade 500 Cream

Mouth: (Girl) RYC Cashsoft DK, shade 501 Sweet (pink). (Boy) RYC Cashsoft DK, shade 509 Lime (green)

Eyelashes: Black embroidery thread

Bow (Girl) Pink gingham ribbon

Hair (Boy): RYC Cashsoft DK, shade 527 Truffle (brown)

F/5 (4 mm) crochet hook

Pair safety eyes

Stuffing

abbreviations

ch *chain;* ***rep*** *repeat;* ***sc*** *single crochet;* ***sc2tog*** *insert hook in st and draw up a loop. Insert hook in next st and draw up another loop. Yarn over, draw through all three loops on hook;* ***ss*** *slip stitch;* ***st(s)*** *stitch(es)*

legs (make 4)

Using either pink or green, make 2ch.
Round 1: 8sc in second ch from hook.
Round 2: 2sc in each st. (16 sts)
Round 3: 1sc in each st.

Change to gray.
Round 4: *1sc in each of next 2 sts, sc2tog; rep from * to end. (12 sts)
Round 5: 1sc in each st until work measures approx 2¼ in. (6 cm).

Fasten off. Stuff.

Pin and sew to body.

tail

• Make 10ch, 2sc in second ch from hook, ss in each ch to end.

Fasten off.

Pin and sew to body. Make a small tassel at bottom end of tail.

face detail

Embroider mouth and eyelashes.

girl

Make a bow and sew to top of head.

boy

Cut several strands approx 2 in. (5 cm) long, knot through loops at top of head, one at a time. Trim.

Opposite: Elliot is obsessed with cars and can't wait until he is old enough to start learning to drive. Until then he has to make do with playing racing games on his computer.

michael storey junior

Michael Storey Junior lives in a tree in his dad's back garden. He has his breakfast in his treehouse and throws bananas at the children next door. His father, Michael Storey, once famously went to Paris and visited all the sights including the Mona Lisa, but he couldn't figure out what she was smiling at.

materials

Head, Body, Arms, Legs, Ears, Tail: Rowan Pure Wool DK, shade 018 Earth (brown)

Muzzle: Rooster Almerino DK shade 202 Hazlenut (light brown)

Eyes: Light brown felt

Scarf: Rowan Pure Wool DK, shade 036 Kiss (red)

RYC Cashsoft DK, shade 509 Lime (light green)

Nose: Black felt

Mouth: Black embroidery thread

F/5 (4 mm) crochet hook

Pair safety eyes

Stuffing

Sewing thread to match felt

abbreviations

ch *chain;* ***rep*** *repeat;* ***sc*** *single crochet;* ***sc2tog*** *insert hook in st and draw up a loop. Insert hook in next st and draw up another loop. Yarn over, draw through all three loops on hook;* ***ss*** *slip stitch;* ***st(s)*** *stitch(es)*

head

- Make 2ch.
- **Round 1:** 6sc in second ch from hook.
- **Round 2:** 2sc in each st. (12 sts)
- **Round 3:** *1sc in next st, 2sc in next st; rep from * to end. (18 sts)
- **Round 4:** *1sc in next 2 sts, 2sc in next st; rep from * to end. (24 sts)
- **Round 5:** *1sc in next 3 sts, 2sc in next st; rep from * to end. (30 sts)
- **Round 6:** *1sc in next 4 sts, 2sc in next st; rep from * to end. (36 sts)
- **Round 7:** 1sc in each st.
- **Round 8:** *1sc in next 4 sts, sc2tog; rep from * to end. (30 sts)
- **Round 9:** *1sc in next 3 sts, sc2tog; rep from * to end. (24 sts)
- **Round 10:** *1sc in next 2 sts, sc2tog; rep from * to end. (18 sts)
- **Round 11:** 1sc in each st.
- **Round 12:** *1sc in next st, sc2tog; rep from * to end.

Cut two small felt circles. Make a small hole in center, insert eyes, push into head and secure. Stuff head. Stitch felt to face.

- **Round 13:** *Miss 1 st, 1sc; rep until opening is closed.

Fasten off.

muzzle

- Make 2ch.
- **Round 1:** 6sc in second ch from hook.
- **Round 2:** 2sc in each st. (12 sts)
- **Rounds 3–4:** 1sc in each st.

Fasten off.

Stuff muzzle and sew to face, overlapping felt.

body

- Make 2ch.
- **Round 1:** 6sc in second ch from hook.
- **Round 2:** 2sc in each st. (12 sts)
- **Round 3:** *1sc in next st, 2sc in next st; rep from * to end. (18 sts)
- **Rounds 4–10:** 1sc in each st.
- **Round 11:** Sc2tog to end.

Fasten off. Stuff.

Pin and sew to head.

arms (make 2)

- Make 2ch.
- **Round 1:** 6sc in second ch from hook.
- **Round 2:** 1sc in each st.

Continue until arms measure 3¼ in. (8 cm)

Fasten off. Do not stuff.

Pin and sew to body.

legs (make 2)

- Make 2ch.
- **Round 1:** 6sc in second ch from hook.
- **Round 2:** 1sc in each st.

Continue until legs measure 1½ in. (4 cm)

Fasten off. Do not stuff.

Pin and sew to body.

ears (make 2)

- Make 2ch.
- **Round 1:** 6sc in second ch from hook.
- **Round 2:** 2sc in each st to end. (12 sts)
- **Round 3:** 1sc in each st.

Fasten off. Pin and sew to head.

tail

- Make 30ch.
- 1sc in second ch from hook, *twist ch and work on other side, miss 1st, 1sc in next st; rep from * to end.

Fasten off.

Pin and sew tail onto body.

face detail

Cut small black felt piece for nose and sew to face.

Embroider mouth detail.

Scarf

Using light green, make 58ch.

- **Row 1:** 1sc in second ch from hook, 1sc in each ch to end.

Fasten off.

- **Row 2:** Using red, 1sc in each st to end.

Fasten off.

oscar the panda

Oscar is a baby panda. He is very special because he's very rare. He lives in China with his parents who eat a lot of bamboo, but Oscar prefers sweet potatoes and popcorn. He is good friends with Bruce the Baby Bear and they sometimes chat to each other on Facebook and play online poker.

head

- Using white, make 2ch.
- **Round 1:** 6sc in second ch from hook.
- **Round 2:** 2sc in each st. (12 sts)
- **Round 3:** *1sc in next st, 2sc in next st; rep from * to end. (18 sts)
- **Round 4:** *1sc in next 2 sts, 2sc in next st; rep from * to end. (24 sts)
- **Round 5:** *1sc in next 3 sts, 2sc in next st; rep from * to end. (30 sts)
- **Round 6:** *1sc in next 4 sts, 2sc in next st; rep from * to end. (36 sts)
- **Round 7:** 1sc in each st.
- **Round 8:** *1sc in next 4 sts, sc2tog; rep from * to end. (30 sts)
- **Round 9:** *1sc in next 3 sts, sc2tog; rep from * to end. (24 sts)
- **Round 10:** *1sc in next 2 sts, sc2tog; rep from * to end. (18 sts)
- **Round 11:** 1sc in each st.
- **Round 12:** *1sc in next st, sc2tog; rep from * to end. (12 sts)

Cut two small circles of white felt, cut two slightly larger black felt circles. Make a small hole in center of each circle. Place white circle on black circle and push safety eyes through center holes, then secure to head. Sew white felt to black felt and black felt to face.

Stuff head firmly.

- **Round 13:** *Miss 1 st, 1sc in next st; rep from * until opening is closed.

Fasten off.

body

- Using white, make 2ch.
- **Round 1:** 6sc in second ch from hook.
- **Round 2:** 2sc in each st. (12 sts)
- **Round 3:** *1sc in next st, 2sc in next st; rep from * to end. (18 sts)

- **Round 4:** 1sc in each st.

Change to black.

- **Rounds 5–7:** 1sc in each st.

Change to white.

- **Rounds 8–10:** 1sc in each st.
- **Round 11:** Sc2tog until opening is closed.

Fasten off. Stuff body firmly. Pin and sew to head.

arms

- Using black, make 2ch.
- **Round 1:** 6sc in second ch from hook.
- **Round 2:** 1sc in each st.

Continue until arms measure 1¼ in. (3 cm).

Fasten off. Do not stuff. Pin and sew to body.

legs

- Using black, make 2ch.
- **Round 1:** 6sc in second ch from hook.
- **Round 2:** 1sc in each st.

Continue until legs measure 1 in. (2.5 cm).

Fasten off. Do not stuff. Pin and sew to body.

ears

- Using black, make 2ch.
- **Round 1:** 6sc in second ch from hook.
- **Round 2:** 2sc in each st to end. (12 sts)
- **Round 3:** 1sc in each st.

Fasten off. Pin and sew to head.

muzzle and nose

Cut circle of black felt for muzzle. Cut a small oval of white felt for nose. Sew nose on muzzle. Embroider mouth with red embroidery thread. Sew onto center of Panda's face.

Tie bow around Panda's neck.

materials

Head, Body: Rowan Pure Wool DK shade 012 (white)

Body, Legs, Arms, Ears: Rowan Pure Wool DK shade 004 (black)

Eyes: Black and white felt

Muzzle: Black felt

Nose: White felt

Mouth: Red embroidery thread

Bow: Green gingham ribbon

F/5 (4 mm) crochet hook

Pair of safety eyes

Stuffing

Sewing thread to match felt

abbreviations

ch *chain;* ***rep*** *repeat;* ***sc*** *single crochet;* ***sc2tog*** *insert hook in st and draw up a loop. Insert hook in next st and draw up another loop. Yarn over, draw through all three loops on hook;* ***st(s)*** *stitch(es)*

kimmie the koala bear

materials

Head, Body, Legs, Arms: Rowan Pure Wool DK, shade 002 Shale (gray)

Rowan Pure Wool DK, shade 012 Snow (white)

Ears: Rowan Kid Silk Haze, shade 634 Cream

Flower: Rowan Pure Wool DK, shade 019 Avocado (green)

Nose: Rowan Pure Wool DK, shade 004 Black

Eyes: White felt

Mouth: Rowan Pure Wool DK, shade 012 Snow (white)

F/5 (4 mm) crochet hook

Pair safety eyes

Stuffing

Sewing thread to match felt

abbreviations

ch *chain;* **rep** *repeat;* **sc** *single crochet;* **sc2tog** *insert hook in st and draw up a loop. Insert hook in next st and draw up another loop. Yarn over, draw through all three loops on hook;* **st(s)** *stitch(es)*

Kimmie came from the Australian Outback, where she used sit all day in the eucalyptus trees getting too sleepy. Now she has moved to a quiet town which has lots of hippies and suits her very well. She tends the plants in her garden and has a stall at the market on Saturday mornings, selling exotic flowers.

head

- Make 2ch.
- **Round 1:** 6sc in second ch from hook.
- **Round 2:** 2sc in each st. (12 sts)
- **Round 3:** *1sc in next st, 2sc in next st; rep from * to end. (18 sts)
- **Round 4:** *1sc in next 2 sts, 2sc in next st; rep from * to end. (24 sts)
- **Round 5:** *1sc in next 3 sts, 2sc in next st; rep from * to end. (30 sts)
- **Round 6:** *1sc in next 4 sts, 2sc in next st; rep from * to end. (36 sts)
- **Round 7:** 1sc in each st.
- **Round 8:** *1sc in next 4 sts, sc2tog; rep from * to end. (30 sts)
- **Round 9:** *1sc in next 3 sts, sc2tog; rep from * to end. (24 sts)
- **Round 10:** *1sc in next 2 sts, sc2tog; rep from * to end. (18 sts)
- **Round 11:** 1sc in each st.
- **Round 12:** *1sc in next st, sc2tog; rep from * to end. (12 sts)

Cut two small felt circles of felt just large enough to show around the eyes. Make a small hole in center of circles and insert safety eyes. Push eyes into face without securing back of eye. Sew felt to face then secure back of safety eye.

- **Round 13:** *Miss 1st, 1sc in next st; rep from * until opening is closed.

Fasten off.

Note: when stuffing the face, push more stuffing in the corners to make a square shape face.

body

- Make 2ch.
- **Round 1:** 6sc in second ch from hook.
- **Round 2:** 2sc in each st. (12 sts)
- **Round 3:** *1sc in next st, 2sc in next st; rep from * to end. (18 sts)
- **Round 4:** *1sc in next 2 sts, 2sc in next st; rep from * to to end. (24 sts)
- **Round 5:** *1sc in next 3 sts, 2sc in next st; rep from * to end. (30 sts)
- **Round 6:** *1sc in next 4 sts, 2sc in next st; rep from * to end. (36 sts)
- **Rounds 7–10:** 1sc in each st.
- **Round 11:** *1sc in next 4 sts, sc2tog; rep from * to end. (30 sts)
- **Round 12:** *1sc in next 3 sts, sc2tog; rep from * to end. (24 sts)
- **Round 13:** *1sc in next 2 sts, sc2tog; rep from * to end. (18 sts)
- **Round 14:** 1sc in each st.

Stuff body firmly.

- **Round 15:** *1sc in next st, sc2tog; rep from * to end. (12 sts)
- **Round 16:** *Miss 1 st, 1sc in next st; rep from * until opening is closed.

Fasten off.

arms

Using white, make 2ch.

- **Round 1:** 9sc in second ch from hook.
- **Round 2:** 1sc in each st.

Change to gray.

- 1sc in each st until arm measures 1½ in. (4 cm).

Fasten off. Stuff lightly. Pin and sew to body.

legs

- Using white, make 2ch.
- **Round 1:** 9sc in second ch from hook.
- **Round 2:** 1sc in each st.

Change to gray.

- 1sc in each st until leg measures 2 in. (5 cm).

Fasten off. Stuff lightly. Pin and sew to body.

ears

- Make 7ch.
- **Row 1:** 1sc in second ch from hook, 1sc in each ch. (6 sts)
- **Row 2:** 1ch, 1sc in each st.

Repeat Row 2 until a square has been formed.

Fasten off.

Fold square in half to form a triangle. Join sides with sc, working 2sc in corner. Fasten off.

Pin and sew to head.

face details

Embroidery a triangular-shaped nose. Embroider mouth. Embroider flower on head.

buzz the emu

Buzz is a private detective and owns an eighties car, a DeLorean. He is very vain and goes to the barbers twice a week. Sometimes he has problems fitting his head in the car, so he has made a hole in the roof to avoid ruining his hairstyle, but he didn't realize what the wind would do to his carefully coiffured locks.

materials

Head: Debbie Bliss Cashmerino DK, shade 019 (blue)

Beak: Debbie Bliss Rialto DK, shade 02 (cream)

Debbie Bliss Rialto DK, shade 14 (light pink)

Neck: Debbie Bliss Rialto DK, shade 11 (orange)

Body, Wings: Rowan Pure Wool DK, shade 042 Dahlia (dark pink)

Legs: Debbie Bliss Rialto DK, shade 09 (green)

Debbie Bliss Rialto DK, shade 02 (cream)

Feet: Black felt

Eyes: Bright green felt

Hair: Rowan Biggy Print, shade 264 Jewel (purple)

Tail feathers: Debbie Bliss Rialto DK, shade 12 (red)

Debbie Bliss Rialto DK, shade 13 (pink)

Debbie Bliss Rialto DK, shade 07 (yellow)

F/5 (4 mm) crochet hook

Pair safety eyes

Stuffing

Sewing thread to match felt

abbreviations

ch *chain;* ***rep*** *repeat;* ***sc*** *single crochet;* ***sc2tog*** *insert hook in st and draw up a loop. Insert hook in next st and draw up another loop. Yarn over, draw through all three loops on hook;* ***ss*** *slip stitch;* ***st(s)*** *stitch(es)*

head

- Make 2ch.
- **Round 1:** 6sc in second ch from hook.
- **Round 2:** 2sc in each st. (12 sts)
- **Round 3:** *1sc in next st, 2sc in next st; rep from * to end. (18 sts)
- **Round 4:** *1sc in next 2 sts, 2sc in next st; rep from * to end. (24 sts)
- **Round 5:** *1sc in next 3 sts, 2sc in next st; rep from * to end. (30 sts)
- **Round 6:** *1sc in next 4 sts, 2sc in next st; rep from * to end. (36 sts)
- **Round 7:** 1sc in each st.
- **Round 8:** *1sc in next 4 sts, sc2tog; rep from * to end. (30 sts)
- **Round 9:** *1sc in next 3 sts, sc2tog; rep from * to end. (24 sts)
- **Round 10:** *1sc in next 2 sts, sc2tog; rep from * to end. (18 sts)
- **Round 11:** 1sc in each st.
- **Round 12:** *1sc in next st, sc2tog; rep from * to end. (12 sts)

Cut two circles of bright green felt. Make a small hole in the centers. Push safety eyes through felt circles and secure in head. Sew felt circles to head.

Stuff firmly.

- **Round 13:** *Miss 1 st, 1sc in next st; rep from * until opening is closed.

Fasten off.

beak (make 2 pieces the same)

- Make 3ch.
- **Row 1:** 1sc in second ch from hook, 1sc in next ch. (2 sts)
- **Row 2:** 2sc in each st. (4 sts)
- **Row 3:** 1sc in each sc.
- **Row 4:** 2sc in first st, 1sc in next 2 sts, 2sc in last st. (6 sts)
- **Row 5:** 1sc in each st.

Change color.

- **Row 6:** 1sc in each st.
- **Row 7:** Sc2tog, 1sc in next 2 sts, sc2tog. (4 sts)
- **Row 8:** 1sc in each st.
- **Row 9:** Sc2tog twice. (2 sts)
- **Row 10:** Sc2tog.

Fasten off. Fold in half. Sew sides. Pin and sew beaks in place on face.

neck

- Make 18ch, ss in first ch to form a ring.
- **Round 1:** 1sc in each ch to end.
- **Rounds 2–7:** 1sc in each st.
- **Rows 8–9:** Ss in first 7 sts, 1sc in last 7 sts.

Fasten off and stuff neck. Pin and sew to back of head.

body

- Make 2ch.
- **Round 1:** 6sc in second ch from hook.
- **Round 2:** 2sc in each st. (12 sts)
- **Round 3:** *1sc in next st, 2sc in next st; rep from * to end. (18 sts)
- **Round 4:** *1sc in next 2 sts, 2sc in next st; rep from * to end. (24 sts)
- **Round 5:** *1sc in next 3 sts, 2sc in next st; rep from * to end. (30 sts)
- **Round 6:** *1sc in next 4 sts, 2sc in next st; rep from * to end. (36 sts)
- **Rounds 7–14:** 1sc in each st.
- **Round 15:** *1sc in next 4 sts, sc2tog; rep from * to end. (30 sts)
- **Round 16:** *1sc in next 3 sts, sc2tog; rep from * to end. (24 sts)
- **Round 17:** *1sc in next 2 sts, sc2tog; rep from * to end. (18 sts)
- **Round 18:** 1sc in each st.

Stuff body firmly.

- **Round 19:** *1sc in next st, sc2tog; rep from * to end.
- **Round 20:** *Miss 1 st, 1sc; rep from * to end. (6 sts)

Fasten off. Pin and sew to neck.

wings (make two)

- Make 13ch.
- **Row 1:** 1sc in second ch from hook, 1sc in each sc. (12 sts)
- **Row 2:** Sc2tog, 1sc in each st to last 2 sts, sc2tog. (10 sts)
- **Row 3:** 1sc in each st.
- **Row 4:** Sc2tog, 1sc in each st to last 2 sts, sc2tog. (8 sts)
- **Row 5:** Sc2tog, 1sc in each st to last 2 sts, sc2tog. (6 sts)
- **Row 6:** 1sc in each st.
- **Row 7:** Sc2tog, 1sc in each st to last 2 sts, sc2tog. (4 sts)
- **Row 8:** Sc2tog twice. (2 sts)
- **Row 9:** Sc2tog.

Fasten off. Pin and sew to body.

legs (make 2)

Worked with wrong side facing.

- Make 2ch.
- **Round 1:** 10sc in second ch from hook.
- **Round 2:** 1sc in each st.

Now change color for each round.

- Rep Round 2 eleven times.

Fasten off. Turn to right side. Stuff firmly. Pin and sew in place.

feet (make two)

Using template, cut four pieces of black felt. Sew pieces together in pairs, leaving an opening at back of foot. Turn inside out, making sure you turn out toes. Stuff lightly and sew up opening. Pin and sew to leg.

tail feathers (make 1 in each color)

- Make 2ch.
- **Round 1:** 6sc in second ch from hook.

Continue to make 1sc in each st until tail measures 2¾ in. (7 cm).

Fasten off. Do not stuff. Pin and sew to body.

alphonso the alpaca

Alphonso owns an Internet business selling Alpaca wool. He lives in a lovely house high in the Andes in Peru and he flies kites in his spare time. His side project is knitting hats and he sells his produce to tourists on their way to the Inca ruins.

materials

Head, Neck, Ears, Body, Legs: Rooster Almerino DK, shade 201 Cornish (cream)

Hooves, Hair: Rooster Almerino DK, shade 202 Hazlenut (light brown)

Muzzle: Beige felt

Nose: Pink felt

Mouth: Dark pink embroidery thread

F/5 (4 mm) crochet hook

Pair safety eyes

Stuffing

abbreviations

ch chain; **hdc(s)** half double(s); **rep** repeat; **sc** single crochet; **sc2tog** insert hook in st and draw up a loop. Insert hook in next st and draw up another loop. Yarn over, draw through all three loops on hook; **ss** slip stitch; **st(s)** stitch(es)

head

- Make 2ch.
- **Round 1:** 6sc in second ch from hook.
- **Round 2:** 2sc in each st. (12 sts)
- **Rounds 3–7:** 1sc in each st.
- **Round 8:** 1sc in each of next 3 sts, 2sc in each of the next 6 sts, 1sc in each of last 3 sts. (18 sts)
- **Round 9:** 1sc in each st.
- **Round 10:** 1sc in each of 6 sts, 2sc in each of next 6 sts, 1sc in last 6 sts.
- **Rounds 11–12:** 1sc in each st.
- **Round 15:** *1sc in next 2 sts, sc2tog; rep from * to end. (18 sts)

Insert safety eyes and secure. Stuff.

- **Round 16:** *1sc in next st, sc2tog; rep from * to end. (12 sts)
- **Round 17:** *Sc2tog; rep from * to end. (6 sts)

Fasten off.

neck

- Make 18ch, ss in first ch to form a ring.
- **Round 1:** 1sc in each ch to end.
- **Rounds 2–8:** 1sc in each st.
- **Rounds 9–10:** Ss in first 9 sts, 1sc in last 9 sts.

Fasten off. Stuff.

Pin and sew neck to back of head.

ears

- Make 6ch.
- 1sc in second ch from hook, 1sc in each ch to last ch, 3sc in last ch, working on other side of ch, 1sc in next 4 sts, ss in first sc.

Fasten off.

body

- Make 2ch.
- **Round 1:** 6sc in second ch from hook.
- **Round 2:** 2sc in each st. (12 sts)
- **Round 3:** *1sc in next st, 2sc in next st; rep from * to end. (18 sts)
- **Round 4:** *1sc in next 2 sts, 2sc in next st; rep from * to end. (24 sts)
- **Round 5:** *1sc in next 3 sts, 2sc in next st; rep from * to end. (30 sts)
- **Round 6:** *1sc in next 4 sts, 2sc in next st; rep from * to end. (36 sts)
- **Rounds 7–14:** 1sc in each st.
- **Round 15:** *1sc in next 4 sts, sc2tog; rep from * to end. (30 sts)
- **Round 16:** *1sc in next 3 sts, sc2tog; rep from * to end. (24 sts)
- **Round 17:** *1sc in next 2 sts, sc2tog; rep from * to end. (18 sts)
- **Round 18:** 1sc in each st.

Stuff.

- **Round 19:** *1sc in next st, sc2tog; rep from * to end.
- **Round 20:** *Miss 1 st, 1sc; rep six times. (6 sts)

Fasten off.

Pin and sew body to head.

legs (make 4)

Using light brown for hooves, make 2ch
- **Round 1:** 6sc in second ch from hook.
- **Round 2:** 2sc in each st. (12 sts)
- **Round 3:** 1sc in each st.

Change to cream.
- **Round 4:** *1sc in each of next 2 sts, sc2tog; rep from * to end. (12 sts)
- **Round 5:** 1sc in each st until leg measures 2 in. (5 cm).

Fasten off. Stuff.

Pin legs in position and sew to body.

tail

- Make 7ch, 2hdc in second ch from hook, 1sc in each st to end.

Fasten off. Pin and sew to body. Cut two short lengths of light brown and knot into end of tail to form a tassle.

face detail

Cut a felt oval for muzzle and a small felt triangle for nose. Sew nose to muzzle. Embroider mouth detail. Pin and sew to face.

hair

Cut 4 in. (10 cm) strands of light brown yarn and knot into top of head, down neck, and across body. Trim hair on head to 1¼ in (3 cm).

vince the rhinestone spider

Vince used to be called Incey Wincey, but now he prefers to be called by his proper name, Vince. His hero is Elvis Presley, although he also likes Neil Diamond. He's an expert piano player due to his eight hands and loves to belt out some rock 'n' roll classics. He tried learning to jive but kept tripping over his feet.

head and body

- Make 2ch.
- **Round 1:** 6sc in second ch from hook.
- **Round 2:** 2sc in each st. (12 sts)
- **Round 3:** *1sc in next st, 2sc in next st; rep from * to end. (18 sts)
- **Round 4:** *1sc in next 2 sts, 2sc in next st; rep from * to end. (24 sts)
- **Round 5:** *1sc in next 3 sts, 2sc in next st; rep from * to end. (30 sts)
- **Rounds 6–10:** 1sc in each st.
- **Round 11:** *1sc in next 3 sts, sc2tog; rep from * to end. (24 sts)
- **Round 12:** *1sc in next 2 sts, sc2tog: rep from * to end. (18 sts)
- **Round 13:** 1sc in each st.

Cut two small circles of white felt, make a small hole in the center, insert safety eyes, push into face and secure. Stuff head.

- **Round 14:** *1sc in next st, sc2tog; rep from * to end. (12 sts)
- **Round 15:** Sc2tog until opening is closed.

Fasten off.

face details

Using white felt and template, cut out mouth. Embroider teeth using black embroidery thread and sew mouth to the face. Embroider pink yarn around the outside to outline lips. Stitch felt eyes in place.

legs (make 8)

- Make 2ch.
- **Round 1:** 4sc in second ch from hook.
- **Round 2:** 2sc in each st. (8 sts)
- **Round 3:** 1sc in each st until each leg measures 2½ in. (6 cm).

Fasten off. Stuff.

Pin legs in position and sew evenly around body.

cowboy hat

- Make 2ch.
- **Round 1:** 6sc in second ch from hook.
- **Round 2:** 2sc in each st. (12 sts)
- **Round 3:** *1sc in next st, 2sc in next st; rep from * to end. (18 sts)
- **Rounds 4–6:** 1sc in each st.
- **Round 7:** 2sc in each st. (36 sts)
- **Round 8:** 2sctog around. (18 sts)
- **Round 9:** *1sc in next st, 2sc in next st; rep from * to end. (27 sts)
- **Round 10:** *1sc in next 2 sts, 2sc in next st; rep from * to end. (36 sts)
- **Round 11:** *1sc in next 3 sts, 2sc in next st; rep from * to end. (45 sts)

Fasten off.

Sew one small silver bead on the end of each leg.

Sew silver beads around the rim of the hat. Curl up brim and hold in place with a single stitch at each side. Put small amount of stuffing inside peak of the hat, then sew hat in place on Spider's head.

materials

Body, Head, Legs: Rowan Pure Wool DK, shade 004 Black

Mouth: White felt, black embroidery thread

Lips: Rowan Pure Wool DK, shade 024 Petal (pink)

Hat: Rowan Pure Wool DK, 012 Snow (white)

Jewels: Small silver beads

F/5 (4 mm) crochet hook

Pair safety eyes

Stuffing

Sewing thread to match felt

abbreviations

ch *chain;* ***rep*** *repeat;* ***sc*** *single crochet;* ***sc2tog*** *insert hook in st and draw up a loop. Insert hook in next st and draw up another loop. Yarn over, draw through all three loops on hook;* ***ss*** *slip stitch;* ***st(s)*** *stitch(es)*

squiddly dudley

Dudley is a sailor; he is a cook in the U.S. Navy. He is extra special because he can work faster than anyone else due to his eight hands. His specialty is chili, it has won several cook-offs, and the sailors all love him because he tells really funny jokes like "What's white and sits in a tree? A refridgerator!"

head and body

- Make 2ch.
- **Round 1:** 6sc in second ch from hook.
- **Round 2:** 2sc in each st. (12 sts)
- **Round 3:** *1sc in next st, 2sc in next st; rep from * to end. (18 sts)
- **Round 4:** *1sc in next 2 sts, 2sc in next st; rep from * to end. (24 sts)
- **Round 5:** *1sc in next 3 sts, 2sc in next st; rep from * to end. (30 sts)
- **Rounds 6–13:** 1sc in each st.
- **Round 14:** *1sc in next 3 sts, sc2tog; rep from * to end. (24 sts)
- **Round 15:** *1sc in next 2 sts, sc2tog; rep from * to end. (18 sts)
- **Round 16:** 1sc in each st.

Insert safety eyes and secure. Stuff firmly.

- **Round 17:** *1sc in next st, sc2tog; rep from * to end. (12 sts)
- **Round 18:** Sc2tog around till opening is closed.

Fasten off.

legs (make 8)

- Make 2ch.
- **Round 1:** 4sc in second ch from hook.
- **Round 2:** 2sc in each st. (8 sts)
- **Round 3:** 1sc in each st until each leg measures 2½ in. (6 cm).

Fasten off. Stuff.

Pin in position and sew to body.

face details

Embroider mouth.

sailor's hat

- Using white, make 2ch.
- **Round 1:** 6sc in second ch from hook.
- **Round 2:** 2sc in each st. (12 sts)
- **Round 3:** *1sc in next st, 2sc in next st; rep from * to end. (18 sts)
- **Rounds 4–6:** 1sc in each st.
- **Round 7:** 2sc in each st. (36 sts)
- **Round 8:** Sc2tog around. (18 sts)
- **Round 9:** *1sc in next st, 2sc in next st; rep from * to end. (27 sts)
- **Round 10:** *1sc in next 2 sts, 2sc in next st; rep from * to end. (36 sts)
- **Round 11:** 1sc in each st to last st, ss.

Fasten off.

Push center of hat up and curl up sides to make a sailor's hat shape.

Embroider anchor on brim.

Sew on to top of head at a jaunty angle.

materials

Head, Body, Legs: Rowan Handknit Cotton shade 318 Seafarer (turquoise)

Hat: Rowan Pure Wool DK, 012 Snow (white)

Hat (anchor): Rowan Pure Wool DK, 007 Cypress (blue)

Mouth: Rowan Pure Wool DK, 036 Kiss (red)

F/5 (4 mm) crochet hook

Pair safety eyes

Stuffing

abbreviations

ch chain; rep repeat; sc single crochet; sc2tog insert hook in st and draw up a loop. Insert hook in next st and draw up another loop. Yarn over, draw through all three loops on hook; ss slip stitch; st(s) stitch(es)

Dudley likes to take a turn at the wheel when the ship comes into port. With his eight arms he can easily steer and wave to all the girls on shore at the same time!

dave the dolphin

Dave lives off the coast of California. He loves surfing with the surfers and spends evenings with them in their Winnebagos chilling out and talking of waves they have surfed around the world. He would like to go to Hawaii for the big waves and hot female dolphins in hula skirts, but he needs to save some cash first.

lower head and body

- Using green and beginning at tip of nose, make 2ch.
- **Row 1:** 2sc in second ch from hook.
- **Rows 2–3:** 1ch, 1sc in each st to end.
- **Row 4:** 1ch, 2sc in next st, 1sc in next st. (3 sts)
- **Row 5:** 1ch, 1sc in each st.
- **Row 6:** 1ch, 2sc in next st, 1sc in next st, 2sc in last st. (5 sts)
- **Row 7:** 1ch, 2sc in next st, 1sc in each of next 3 sts, 2sc in last st. (7 sts)
- **Row 8:** 1ch, 2sc in next st, 1sc in next 5 sts, 2sc in last st. (9 sts)
- **Row 9:** 1ch, 1sc in each st to end.
- **Row 10:** 1ch, 2sc in first st, 1sc in each of next 7 sts, 2sc in last st. (11 sts)
- **Rows 11–27:** 1ch, 1sc in each st to end.
- **Row 28:** 1ch, sc2tog, 1sc in each of next 7 sts, sc2tog. (9 sts)
- **Rows 29–30:** 1ch, 1sc in each st to end.
- **Row 31:** 1ch, sc2tog, 1sc in each of next 5 sts, sc2tog. (7 sts)
- **Rows 32–33:** 1ch 1sc in each st to end.
- **Row 34:** 1ch, sc2tog, 1sc in each of next 3 sts,

materials

Lower Head and Body: RYC Cashsoft DK, shade 509 Lime (light green)

Upper Head and Body, Tail, Fins, Flippers: RYC Cashsoft DK, shade 504 Glacier (light blue)

F/5 (4 mm) crochet hook

Pair safety eyes

Stuffing

abbreviations

ch *chain;* ***sc*** *single crochet;* ***sc2tog*** *insert hook in st and draw up a loop. Insert hook in next st and draw up another loop. Yarn over, draw through all three loops on hook;* ***hdc*** *half double;* ***rem*** *remaining;* ***rep*** *repeat;* ***ss*** *slip stitch;* ***st(s)*** *stitch(es);* ***dc*** *double*

sc2tog. (5 sts)
- **Rows 35–46:** 1ch, 1sc in each st to end.
- **Row 47:** 1ch, 1sc in each st to end, 9ch.

tail

- **Row 48:** Ss in second ch from hook, 1sc in each of next 2 ch, 1hdc in next ch, 1dc in each of next 4 ch, 1dc in each of next 5 sts, 9ch, turn, ss in second ch from hook, 1sc in each of next 2 ch, 1hdc in next ch, 1dc in each of next 4 ch. Twisting second half of tail so that top of sts face nose end of body, ss in end of Row 47.

Fasten off.

upper head and body

- Using blue and beginning at tip of nose, make 2ch.
- **Row 1:** 1ch, 2sc in second ch from hook.
- **Row 2:** 1ch, 1sc in each st to end. (2 sts)
- **Row 3:** 1ch, 2sc in first st, 1sc in next st. (3 sts)
- **Row 4:** 1ch, 1sc in first st, 2sc in next st, 1sc in last st. (4 sts)
- **Row 5:** 1ch, 1sc in first st, 2sc in each of next 2 sts, 1sc in last st. (6 sts)
- **Row 6:** 1ch, 1 sc in first st, 2sc in each of next 4 sts, 1sc in last sts. (10 sts)
- **Row 7:** 1ch, 1sc in first st, 2sc in each of next 8 sts, 1sc in last st. (18 sts)
- **Rows 8–10:** 1ch, 1sc in each st.
- **Row 11:** 1ch, 1sc in each of first 8 sts, 2sc in each of next 2 sts, 1sc in each of last 8 sts (20 sts)
- **Rows 12–16:** 1ch, 1sc in each st.
- **Row 17:** 1ch, 1sc in each of first 8 sts, 2sc in each of next 4 sts, 1sc in each of last 8 sts (24 sts)
- **Rows 18–20:** 1ch, 1sc in each st.
- **Row 21:** 1ch, sc2tog, 1sc in each of next 20 sts, sc2tog. (22 sts)
- **Row 22:** 1ch, sc2tog, 1sc in each of next 18 sts, sc2tog. (20 sts)
- **Row 23:** 1ch, 1sc in each st.
- **Row 24:** 1ch, sc2tog, 1sc in each of next 16 sts, sc2tog. (18 sts)
- **Row 25:** 1ch, 1sc in each st.
- **Row 26:** 1ch, sc2tog, 1sc in each of next 14 sts, sc2tog. (16 sts)
- **Rows 27–28:** 1ch, 1sc in each st.
- **Row 29:** 1ch, sc2tog, 1sc in each of next 12 sts, sc2tog. (14 sts)
- **Row 30:** 1ch, 1sc in each st.
- **Row 31:** 1ch, sc2tog, 1sc in each of next 10 sts, sc2tog. (12 sts)
- **Row 32:** 1ch, sc2tog, 1sc in each of next 8 sts, sc2tog. (10 sts)
- **Rows 33–34:** 1ch, 1sc in each st.
- **Row 35:** 1ch, sc2tog, 1sc in each of next 6 sts, sc2tog. (8 sts)
- **Rows 36–45:** 1ch, 1sc in each st.
- **Row 46:** 1ch, sc2tog, 1sc in each of next 4 sts, sc2tog. (6 sts)
- **Row 47:** 1ch, 1sc in each of first 2 sts, sc2tog, 1sc in each of last 2 sts, 9ch.

tail

- **Row 48:** Ss in second ch from hook, 1sc in each of next 2 ch, 1hdc in next ch, 1dc in each of next 4 ch, 1dc in each of next 5 sts, 9ch, turn. Ss in second ch from hook, 1sc in each of next 2ch, 1hdc in next ch. 1dc in each

of next 4ch. Twisting second half of tail as before, ss in end st of Row 47. Fasten off.

Using blue sew lower head and body to upper head and body. Starting at Row 30 work around tail end to opposite side of Row 30. Secure safety eyes, approx 2 in. (5 cm) apart. Stuff body and continue stuffing while sewing remainder together.

top fin (make 2)

- Using blue and starting at base of fin, make 9ch.
- **Row 1:** 1sc in second ch from hook, 1sc in each ch to end. (8 sts)
- **Row 2:** 1ch, 1sc in each st.
- **Row 3:** 1ch, sc2tog twice, 1sc in each of next 4 sts. (6 sts)
- **Row 4:** 1ch, 1sc in each of first 4 sts, sc2tog. (5 sts)
- **Row 5:** 1ch, sc2tog, 1sc in each of next 3 sts. (4 sts)
- **Row 6:** 1ch, 1sc in each of first 2 sts, sc2tog. (3 sts)
- **Row 7:** 1ch, 2sc in first st, 1sc in each of next 2 sts. (4 sts)
- **Row 8:** 1ch, sc2tog, 1sc in next st, 2sc in last st. (4 sts)
- **Row 9:** 1ch, 2sc in first st, 1sc in next st, sc2tog. (4 sts)
- **Row 10:** 1ch, sc2tog, 1sc in next st, 3sc in last st. (5 sts)
Fasten off.

Sew two fins together, matching sts around three sides and leaving bottom of fin open. Stuff lightly. With fin curving toward tail, sew fin to center back of upper body approx 6 in. (15 cm) back from tip of nose.

flippers (make 2)

- Using blue and starting at the tip of the fin, make 6ch.
- **Round 1:** 1sc in second ch from hook, 1sc in each of next 3 sts, 2sc in next st, working across opposite side of foundation ch, 1sc in each of next 4 sts, do not join. (10 sts)

Continue working in a spiral marking beginning of each round with a stitch marker or length of contrasting yarn.

- **Round 2:** 1ch, 1sc in each st. (10 sts)
- **Round 3:** 1ch *2sc in first st, 1sc in each of next 4 sts; rep from * once. (12 sts)
- **Rounds 4–7:** 1ch, 1sc in each st.
- **Round 8:** 1ch, *2sc in first st, 1sc in each of next 5 sts; rep from * once. (14 sts)
- **Round 9:** 1ch, 1sc in each st.

Fasten off.

Flatten out flippers and sew one on seam at each side of body approx 3 in. (8 cm) from tip of nose.

the fish brothers

The Fish Brothers are in a ska band and they tour around the world. Martin is the drummer, he is more traditional than Jonti and he likes blue and green. Jonti likes bright colors, particularly pink; it reflects well on stage. Even though he's in a ska band, he secretly loves show tunes and would much rather be treading the boards in a Broadway musical—his dream would be to star in *The Sound of Music*.

materials

Blue fish

Face, Fins, Tail: Rowan Handknit Cotton, shade 322 Mojito (green)

Body: Rowan Handknit Cotton, shade 324 Bermuda (mid blue)
Rowan Handknit Cotton, shade 327 Aqua, (light blue)

Eyes: Orange felt

Mouth: Red embroidery thread

Pink fish

Face, Fins, Tail: Rooster Almerino Aran, shade 307 Brighton Rock (pink)

Body: Debbie Bliss Cashmerino DK, shade 026 (yellow)
Debbie Bliss Cashmerino DK, shade 023 (apricot)

Eyes: Lilac felt

Mouth: Rowan Handknit Cotton, shade 324 Bermuda (mid blue)

Both fish

F/5 (4 mm) crochet hook

Pair safety eyes

Stuffing

Sewing thread to match felt

abbreviations

ch chain; ***sc*** single crochet; ***sc2tog*** insert hook in st and draw up a loop. Insert hook in next st and draw up another loop. Yarn over, draw through all three loops on hook; ***rep*** repeat; ***ss*** slip stitch; ***st(s)*** stitch(es); ***dc*** double

face and body

- Make 2ch.
- **Round 1:** 8sc in second ch from hook.
- **Round 2:** 2sc in each st. (16 sts)
- **Rounds 3–5:** 1sc in each st.
- **Round 6:** 1sc in next st, *1sc in next 2 sts, 2sc in next st; rep from * to end. (21 sts)
- **Round 7:** 1sc in each st.
- **Round 8:** 1sc in next st, *sc2tog, 1sc in next 2 sts; rep from * to end. (16 sts)

Change to first body color.

- **Round 9:** *Miss 1 st, 5dc in next st, ss in next st; rep from * to end working last ss in top of first dc.

Change color to second body color.

- **Round 10:** 5dc in top of next ss, *ss in top of third dc from previous round; rep from * to end.
- **Round 11:** With first body color, *ss in top of third dc from previous round, 5dc in ss; rep from * to last st, ss in first ss.

Rep Rounds 9–10 until work measures 6 in. (15 cm) from start.

Change color to next body color.

- **Next round:** *Ss in top of third dc from previous round, 3dc in ss; rep from * to end.
- **Next round:** *Ss in top of center dc, 1dc in next ss; rep from * to end. (10 sts)
- **Next round:** 1sc in each st.

Cut two small felt circles for back of eyes. Make a hole in each center, push safety eye through hole. Insert into face and secure. Sew felt circles in place.

Stuff.

- **Last round:** *Miss 1st, 1sc in next st; rep from * until opening is closed.

Fasten off.

face detail

Embroider mouth onto face.

tail fins (make 2)

- Make 2ch. Worked with wrong side facing.
- **Round 1:** 6sc in second ch from hook.
- **Round 2:** 2sc in each st. (12 sts)
- **Round 3:** 1sc in each st.
- **Round 4:** *1sc in next 2 sts, sc2tog; rep from * to end. (9 sts)
- **Rounds 5–10:** 1sc in each st.

Fasten off. Turn to right side. Stuff very lightly.

Pin and sew to body.

side fins (make 2)

- Make 11ch.
- **Row 1:** Ss in second ch from hook, 1sc in each of next 9ch, turn.
- **Row 2:** 1sc in next 8 sts, ss in next 2 sts, turn.
- **Row 3:** Ss in next st, 1sc in each st to end.

Fasten off

Pin and sew fins to body.

top fin

- Make 11ch, ss in second ch from hook. *4ch, ss in second ch from hook, ss in each of next 2ch, ss in next ch; rep from * until you have nine spikes, ss in last ch.

Fasten off.

Pin lengthways along top of fish so spikes stick up. Sew in place.

freddie the seal

Freddie lives in New Orleans near the aquarium and has a job cleaning up trash from the Mississippi; he likes to do his bit for the environment. A long time ago he used to wear jeans with lumberjack shirts to work and used to have bigger whiskers, which he now keeps trimmed so the fish don't get stuck in them.

materials

Head, Body, Tail, Fins: Rowan Pure Wool DK, shade 005 Glacier (light blue)

Mouth: Rowan Pure Wool DK, shade 012 Snow (white)

Nose, Whiskers: Rowan Pure Wool DK, shade 004 Black

F/5 (4 mm) crochet hook

Pair safety eyes

Stuffing

abbreviations

ch chain; sc single crochet; sc2tog insert hook in st and draw up a loop. Insert hook in next st and draw up another loop. Yarn over, draw through all three loops on hook; rep repeat; ss slip stitch; st(s) stitch(es); dc double

lower head and body

- Make 2ch.
- **Row 1:** 2sc in second ch from hook.
- **Rows 2–3:** 1ch, 1sc in each st to end.
- **Row 4:** 1ch, 2sc in next st, 1sc in next st. (3 sts)
- **Row 5:** 1ch, 1sc in next 3 sts.
- **Row 6:** 1ch, 2sc in next st, 1sc in next st, 2sc in last st. (5 sts)
- **Row 7:** 1ch, 2sc in next st, 1sc in each of next 3 sts, 2sc in last st. (7 sts)
- **Row 8:** 1ch, 2sc in next st, 1sc in next 5 sts, 2sc in last st. (9 sts)
- **Row 9:** 1ch, 1sc in each st to end.
- **Row 10:** 1ch, 2sc in next st, 1sc in each of next 7 sts, 2sc in last st. (11 sts)
- **Rows 11–27:** 1ch, 1sc in each st to end.
- **Row 28:** 1ch, sc2tog, 1sc in each of next 7 sts, sc2tog. (9 sts)
- **Rows 29–30:** 1ch, 1sc in each st to end.
- **Row 31:** 1ch, sc2tog, 1sc in each of next 5 sts, sc2tog. (7 sts)
- **Rows 32–33:** 1ch, 1sc in each st to end.
- **Row 34:** 1ch, sc2tog, 1sc in each of next 3 sts, sc2tog. (5 sts)
- **Rows 35–39:** 1ch, 1sc in each st to end.
- **Row 40:** 1ch, 1sc in each st to end, 6ch.

Do not fasten off.

lower tail

- 1dc in third ch from hook, 1dc in each of next 3ch, ss in second sc, ss in next 2sc, 6ch, 1dc in third ch from hook, 1dc in next 3ch, ss in last sc.

Fasten off.

upper body

- Make 4ch.
- **Row 1:** 4sc in second ch from hook.
- **Rows 2–5:** 1ch, 1sc in each st to end. (4 sts)
- **Row 6:** 1ch, 1sc in next st, 2sc in next st, 1sc in next 2 sts. (5 sts)
- **Row 7:** 1ch, 2sc in next st, 1sc in each of next 3 sts, 2sc in last st. (7 sts)
- **Row 8:** 1ch, 2sc in next st, 1sc in next 5 sts, 2sc in last st. (9 sts)
- **Row 9:** 1ch, 1sc in each st to end.
- **Row 10:** 1ch, 2sc in first st, 1sc in each of next 7 sts, 2sc in last st. (11 sts)
- **Rows 11–27:** 1ch, 1sc in each st to end.
- **Row 28:** 1ch, sc2tog, 1sc in each of next 7 sts, sc2tog. (9 sts)
- **Rows 29–30:** 1ch, 1sc in each st to end.
- **Row 31:** 1ch, sc2tog, 1sc in each of next 5 sts, sc2tog. (7 sts)
- **Rows 32–33:** 1ch, 1sc in each st to end.
- **Row 34:** 1ch, sc2tog, 1sc in each of next 3 sts, sc2tog. (5 sts)
- **Rows 35–39:** 1ch, 1sc in each st to end.
- **Row 40:** 1ch, 1sc in each st to end, 6ch, turn.

Do not fasten off.

upper tail

- 1dc in third ch from hook, 1dc in each of next 3ch, ss in second sc, ss in next 2sc, 6ch, 1dc in third ch from hook, 1dc in next 3ch, ss in last sc.

Fasten off.

fins

- Make 5ch.
- **Row 1:** 1sc in second ch from hook, 1sc in each of next 3ch. (4 sts)
- **Rows 2–8:** 1ch, 1sc in each st.
- **Row 9:** 1ch, sc2tog, 1sc in next sc. (3 sts)
- **Row 10:** 1ch, 1sc in each st.
- **Row 11:** 1ch, sc2tog, 1sc in next sc. (2 sts)
- **Row 12:** 1ch, 1sc in each st.
- **Row 13:** 1ch, sc2tog.

Fasten off.

Pin upper and lower body together, start sewing from center of body toward the tail, sew the tails together, then sew along other side to within 2 in. (5 cm) of start of seam. Insert safety eyes and secure. Stuff, beginning at tail end. Sew opening together. Sew on side fins.

face detail

Cut strands of black yarn and knot through stitches at side of nose to make whiskers.

Embroider nose and mouth.

festive favorites

Join in the Christmas fun. Blossom the Fairy has knocked the candy canes off the table and Ralph the Reindeer has crash-landed on the roof. Luckily, Sparkles the Snowman has organized the carols and they're all ready to start crooning his latest composition: "Ralph the Red-Nosed Reindeer."

Ralph

Blossom

Sparkles

ralph the red nose reindeer

Ralph is Rudolph's cousin; he is the only other reindeer to have a red nose. He's very excited because he's going to assist Santa this year for the very first time. He hasn't yet perfected his landing technique and keeps crashing on his practice flights. On his days off he plays water polo, which is pretty brave considering the water temperatures up in the North Pole.

materials

Head, Body, Tail: Rooster Almerino DK, 202 Hazelnut (light brown)

Antlers: Rooster Almerino DK, 201 Cornish (cream)

Scarf: Rooster Almerino DK, 207 Gooseberry (green)

Nose: Rooster Almerino Aran, 310 Rooster (red)

2 bells (do not use if toy is for a child under 3 years old)

F/5 (4 mm) crochet hook

Pair of safety eyes

Stuffing

abbreviations

ch *chain;* ***rep*** *repeat;* ***sc*** *single crochet;* ***sc2tog*** *insert hook in st and draw up a loop. Insert hook in next st and draw up another loop. Yarn over, draw through all three loops on hook;* ***ss*** *slip stitch;* ***st(s)*** *stitch(es)*

head

- Make 2ch.
- **Round 1:** 6sc in second ch from hook.
- **Round 2:** 2sc in each st. (12 sts)
- **Rounds 3–5:** 1sc in each st.
- **Round 6:** 1sc in each of next 3 sts, 2sc in each of next 6 sts, 1sc in each of last 3 sts. (18 sts)
- **Round 7:** 1sc in each st.
- **Round 8:** 1sc in first 6 sts, 2sc in each of next 6 sts, 1sc in last 6 sts. (24 sts)
- **Round 9:** 1sc in each st.
- **Round 10:** *1sc in next 2 sts, sc2tog; rep from * to end. (18 sts)

Insert eyes and secure. Stuff.

- **Round 11:** *1sc in next st, sc2tog; rep from * to end. (12 sts)
- **Round 12:** Sc2tog to end. (6 sts)

Fasten off.

antlers (make 2)

- Make 2ch.
- **Round 1:** 6sc in second ch from hook.
- **Round 2:** 1sc in each st.

Continue until antler measures approx 2 in. (5 cm).

Fasten off. Stuff.

antler branches (make 2)

- Make as Antlers, working until piece measures 1 in. (2.5 cm) long.

Fasten off. Do not stuff.

Pin and sew Antlers to center of head between ears. Pin and sew Antler Branch ½ in. (1 cm) up from base of outer edge of each Antler.

neck

- Make 18ch, ss in first ch to form a ring.
- **Round 1:** 1sc in each ch.
- **Rounds 2–6:** 1sc in each st.
- **Rounds 7–8:** Ss in first 9 sts, 1sc in each of last 9 sts.

Fasten off. Stuff.

Pin and sew shaped edge to back of head.

body

- Make 2ch.
- **Round 1:** 6sc in second ch from hook.
- **Round 2:** 2sc in each st. (12 sts)
- **Round 3:** *1sc in next st, 2sc in next st; rep from * to end. (18 sts)
- **Round 4:** *1sc in next 2 sts, 2sc in next st; rep from * to end. (24 sts)
- **Rounds 5–19:** 1sc in each st.

- **Round 20:** *1sc in next 4 sts, sc2tog; rep from * to end. (20 sts)
- **Round 21:** *1sc in next 3 sts, sc2tog; rep from * to end. (16 sts)
- **Round 22:** *1sc in next 2 sts. sc2tog; rep from * to end. (12 sts)

Stuff body.

- **Round 23:** Sc2tog until opening is closed.

Fasten off. Pin and sew to neck.

ears (make 2)

- Make 4ch.
- 1sc in second ch from hook, 1sc in next ch, 3sc in last ch, working in other side of ch, 1sc in next 2 sts, ss in first sc.

Fasten off. Pin and sew to head.

legs (make 4)

Worked with wrong side facing.

- Using cream for hooves, make 2ch.
- **Round 1:** 6sc in second ch from hook.
- **Round 2:** 2sc in each st. (12 sts)
- **Round 3:** *1sc in next st, 2sc in next st; rep from * to end. (18 sts)
- **Round 4:** 1sc in back of each st.

Change to light brown. Continue in stripes of two rounds light brown and two rounds cream.

- **Round 5:** 1sc in each st.
- **Round 6:** *1sc in next st, sc2tog; rep from * to end. (12 sts)
- **Rounds 7–18:** 1sc in each st.

Turn to right side. Stuff lightly.

- **Round 19:** Sc2tog to end.

Pin and sew to body.

tail

- Make 7ch.
- 1sc in each ch to end. Fasten off.

Pin and sew to body.

scarf

- Make 50ch.
- **Row 1:** 1sc in each ch to end.
- **Row 2:** 1sc in each st.

Fasten off. Attach bell to each end, if used, and tie round neck.

face details

Embroider nose.

sparkles the snowman

Sparkles is a singer; he sings all the old Frank Sinatra and Dean Martin songs, and has recently discovered the band Snow Patrol. His favorite song is Dean Martin's "I've Got The Sun In The Morning." He's very concerned about global warming and is currently trying to block the hole in the ozone with chewing gum.

materials

Head, Body, Arms: Rowan Pure Wool DK, shade 012 Snow (white)

Buttons: Rowan Pure Wool DK, shade 004 Black

Nose: Rowan Pure Wool DK, shade 040 Tangerine (orange)

Mouth: Rowan Pure Wool DK, shade 041 Scarlet (red)

Scarf: Rooster Almerino DK, shade 202 Hazelnut (light brown)
Rooster Almerino DK, shade 207 Gooseberry (green)

Hat: Rooster Almerino DK, shade 202 Hazelnut (light brown)

F/5 (4 mm) crochet hook

Stuffing

Pair safety eyes

2 bells (not suitable for young children)

abbreviations

ch chain; **rep** repeat; **sc** single crochet; **sc2tog** insert hook in st and draw up a loop. Insert hook in next st and draw up another loop. Yarn over, draw through all three loops on hook; **ss** slip stitch; **st(s)** stitch(es)

head

- Make 2ch.
- **Round 1:** 6sc in second ch from hook.
- **Round 2:** 2sc in each st. (12 sts)
- **Round 3:** *1sc in next st, 2sc in next st; rep from * to end. (18 sts)
- **Round 4:** *1sc in next 2 sts, 2sc in next st; rep from * to end. (24 sts)
- **Round 5:** *1sc in next 3 sts, 2sc in next st; rep from * to end. (30 sts)
- **Rounds 6–10:** 1sc in each st.
- **Round 11:** 1sc in next 3 sts, sc2tog; rep from * to end. (24 sts)
- **Round 12:** *1sc in next 2 sts, sc2tog; rep from * to end. (18 sts)

Insert safety eyes and secure. Stuff.

- **Round 13:** *1sc in next st, sc2tog; rep from * to end.
- **Round 15:** Sc2tog until opening is closed.

Fasten off.

body

- Make 2ch.
- **Round 1:** 6sc in second ch from hook.
- **Round 2:** 2sc in each st. (12 sts)
- **Round 3:** *1sc in next st, 2sc in next st; rep from * to end. (18 sts)
- **Round 4:** *1sc in next 2 sts, 2sc in next st; rep from * to end. (24 sts)
- **Round 5:** *1sc in next 3 sts, 2sc in next st; rep from * to end. (30 sts)
- **Round 6:** *1sc in next 4 sts, 2sc in next st; rep from * to end. (36 sts)
- **Rounds 7–14:** 1sc in each st.
- **Round 15:** *1sc in next 4 sts, sc2tog; rep from * to end. (30 sts)
- **Round 16:** *1sc in next 3 sts, sc2tog; rep from * to end. (24 sts)

- **Round 17:** *1sc in next 2 sts, sc2tog; rep from * to end. (18 sts)
- **Round 18:** 1sc in each st.

Stuff body firmly.

- **Round 19:** *1sc in next st, sc2tog; rep from * to end.
- **Round 20:** *Miss 1st, 1sc in next st; rep from * to end. (6 sts)

Fasten off.

Pin and sew to head.

Using black, work three French knots down center of body for buttons.

arms (make 2)

- Make 2ch.
- **Round 1:** 6sc in second ch from hook.
- **Round 2:** 1sc in each st.
- Continue until arms measure 1½ in. (4 cm).

Fasten off. Do not stuff.

Pin and sew arms to body.

nose

- Using, orange, make 2ch.
- **Round 1:** 6sc in second ch from hook.
- **Round 2:** 1sc in each st.
- **Round 3:** Sc2tog 3 times.
- **Round 4:** *Insert hook into next st and draw up a loop; rep from * twice more, yarn over and draw through all 4 loops.

Fasten off. Do not stuff.

Pin and sew to face.

face details

Embroider mouth.

scarf

Using green, make 5ch.
- **Row 1:** 1sc in second ch from hook, 1sc in next 3 sts. (4 sts)
- **Row 2:** 1ch, 1sc in each st. (4 sts)

Join in light brown.
- **Row 3:** 1ch, 1sc in each st.
- **Row 4:** 1ch, 1sc in each st.

Join in green.
- **Row 5:** 1ch, 1sc in each st.

Rep Rows 3–5 until scarf measures 11½ in. (29 cm)

Fasten off.

Sew a bell on each end. Tie scarf round neck.

hat

- Using light brown, make 2ch.
- **Round 1:** 6ch in second ch from hook.
- **Round 2:** 2sc in each st. (12 sts)
- **Round 3:** *1sc in next st, 2sc in next st; rep from * to end. (18 sts)
- **Rounds 4–6:** 1sc in each st.
- **Round 7:** 2sc in each st. (36 sts)
- **Round 8:** Sc2tog to end. (18 sts)
- **Round 9:** *1sc in next st, 2sc in next st; rep from * to end. (27 sts)
- **Round 10:** *1sc in next 2 sts, 2sc in next st; rep from * to end. (36 sts)
- **Round 11:** *1sc in next 3 sts, 2sc in next st; rep from * to last st, ss in last st. (45 sts)

Fasten off.

Put hat on head and make small stitches into head to secure in place.

blossom the fairy

Blossom is a very clumsy fairy and is always knocking things over with her wings. She sometimes rides Camilla the Pony and she falls off even before Camilla has started walking. She never gets upset when she bumps into objects, she just laughs. Sometimes she's the Christmas Fairy and is good friends with Ralph the Reindeer.

head

- Make 2ch.
- **Round 1:** 6sc in second ch from hook.
- **Round 2:** 2sc in each st. (12 sts)
- **Round 3:** *1sc in next st, 2sc in next st; rep from * to end. (18 sts)
- **Round 4:** *1sc in next 2 sts, 2sc in next st; rep from * to end. (24 sts)
- **Rounds 5–8:** 1sc in each st.
- **Round 9:** *1sc in next 2 sts, sc2tog; rep from * to end. (18 sts)
- **Round 10:** *1sc in next st, sc2tog; rep from * to end. (12 sts)

Insert eyes and secure. Stuff.

- **Round 11:** Sc2tog until opening is closed.

Fasten off.

body

- Make 2ch.
- **Round 1:** 6sc in second ch from hook.
- **Round 2:** 2sc in each st. (12 sts)
- **Round 3:** *1sc in next st, 2sc in next st; rep from * to end. (18 sts)
- **Rounds 4–10:** 1sc in each st.

Stuff body lightly.

- **Round 12:** *1sc in next st, sc2tog; rep from * to end. (12 sts)
- **Round 13:** Sc2tog until opening is closed.

Fasten off. Stuff.

Pin and sew to head.

legs (make 2)

Using blue for shoes, make 2ch.

- **Round 1:** 6sc in second ch from hook.
- **Round 2:** *1sc in next st, 2sc in next st; rep from * to end. (9 sts)
- **Round 3:** 1sc in each st.

Change to beige.

- **Rounds 4–12:** 1sc in each st.

Fasten off. Stuff.

Pin and sew to body.

Attach a bell to the top of each shoe. (Do not use bells if giving toy to a small child.)

arms (make 2)

Using beige, make 2ch.

- **Round 1:** 5sc in second ch from hook.
- **Round 2:** *1sc in next st, 2sc in next st; rep from * once, 1sc in last st. (7 sts)
- **Rounds 3–10:** 1sc in each st.

Fasten off. Stuff.

Pin and sew to body.

materials

Head, Body, Legs, Arms: Wendy Mode DK, shade 203 (beige)

Shoes: Rooster Almerino Aran, shade 302 Sugared Almond (blue)

Dress, Mouth: Debbie Bliss Cashmerino DK, 05 (pink)

Hair: Rooster Almerino DK, shade 203 Strawberry Cream (light pink)

Wings: Rooster Almerino DK, shade 201 Cornish (cream)

Bow: Silver ribbon

2 Bells (not suitable for young children)

F/5 (4 mm) crochet hook

Pair safety eyes

Stuffing

abbreviations

ch *chain;* ***dc*** *double;* ***rep*** *repeat;* ***sc*** *single crochet;* ***sc2tog*** *insert hook in st and draw up a loop. Insert hook in next st and draw up another loop. Yarn over, draw through all three loops on hook;* ***ss*** *slip stitch;* ***st(s)*** *stitch(es)*

dress

- Make 30ch, ss in first ch to form a ring.
- **Rounds 1–4:** 1sc in each st. (30 sts)
- **Round 5:** Sc2tog, 1sc in next 14 sts, sc2tog, 1sc in each st to end. (28 sts)
- **Round 6:** Sc2tog, 1sc in next 13 sts, sc2tog, 1sc in each st to end. (26 sts)
- **Rounds 7–9:** 1sc in each st.
- **Round 10:** Sc2tog, 1sc in next 12 sts, sc2tog, 1sc in each st to end. (24 sts)
- **Round 11:** Sc2tog, 1sc in next 11 sts, sc2tog, 1sc in each st to end. (22 sts)

Fasten off.

bottom of dress

Turn dress upside down. Join yarn at start of round.

- **Round 1:** 2sc in first st, 1sc in next 14 sts, 2sc in next st, 1sc in each st to end. (32 sts)
- **Round 2:** 2sc in first st, 1sc in next 15 sts, 2sc in next st, 1sc in each st to end. (34 sts)
- **Rounds 3–4:** 1sc in each st (at end of Round 4 ss in first st).

Fasten off.

Left shoulder

Turn dress right way up and working on top of dress with fasten off point on your right, join yarn in third st in towards the center, turn.

- **Row 1:** 1sc in next 3 sts. (3 sts)
- **Row 2:** 1sc in next 2 sts. (2 sts)
- **Row 3:** Sc2tog. (1 st)
- **Row 4:** 1sc.
- **Row 5:** 2sc in st. (2 sts)
- **Row 6:** 1sc in next 2 sts, turn. (2 sts)
- **Row 7:** 2sc in next st, make 1sc in next st. (3 sts)

Fasten off.

Right shoulder

Miss 3 sts after left shoulder, join yarn to next st. Work as left shoulder.

Try dress on Fairy, pin and sew straps in place at back of dress.

face detail

Embroider mouth.

hair

Cut enough 10 in. (25 cm) long strands of light pink yarn to cover top of head. Place width ways across top and round back of head. Using a wool sewing needle and light pink yarn, make small backstitches from the front of the head to the back to secure the strands in place. Tie bunches with bows of silver ribbon.

wings (make 2)

- Make 9ch.
- **Row 1:** 1sc in second ch from hook, 1sc in each ch. (8 sts)
- **Row 2:** 2sc in next st, 1sc in each st to last st, 2sc in last st. (10 sts)
- **Row 3:** 1sc in each st.
- **Row 4:** 2sc in next st, 1sc in each st to last st, 2sc in last st. (12 sts)
- **Row 5:** 1sc in each st.
- **Row 6:** 2sc in next st, 1sc in each st to last st, 2sc in last st. (14 sts)

Fasten off.

wing edging

Rejoin yarn at beginning of first row.

- **Round 1:** 1ch, 1sc in each row-end, 3sc in corner, 1sc in each st, 3sc in corner, 1sc in each row-end, 2sc in corner, 1sc in each ch, 1sc in same place as first sc, ss in first sc.
- **Round 2:** 3ch, miss first sc, *1dc in each sc to corner, 5dc in center sc at corner; rep from * once, 1dc in each sc to corner.

Fasten off.

Pin and sew shortest edge of wings lengthways onto back of Fairy.

Edge three sides of each wing with silver ribbon.

techniques

In this section, we explain how to master the simple crochet techniques that you need to make the toys in this book.

making a slip knot

The simplest way is to make a circle with the yarn so that the loop is facing downward.

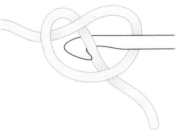

1. Hold circle at the top where the yarn crosses in one hand and let the tail drop down so it falls in the center of the circle. With your hook pull the tail through the circle and pull the knot so it tightens loosely.

2. Put the hook into the circle and pull the knot gently so it forms a loose loop on the hook.

holding yarn

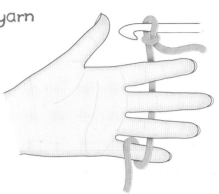

Pick up the yarn with your little finger in the opposite hand to your hook, with your palm facing upward. Turn your hand to face downward with the yarn on top of your index finger and under the other two fingers and

wrapped right round the little finger. Keeping your index finger only at a slight curve, hold your work just under the slip knot with the other hand.

holding the hook

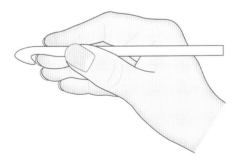

Pick up your hook as though you were picking up a pen or pencil. Keeping the hook held loosely between your fingers and thumb, turn your hand so the palm is facing

up and the hook is balanced in your hand and is resting in the space between your index finger and your thumb.

yarn around hook

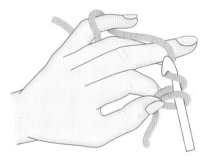

To create a stitch, you'll need to catch the yarn with the hook and pull it through the loop. Holding your yarn and hook correctly, catch the yarn from behind with the hook pointed upward. As you gently pull the yarn through the loop on the hook, turn

the hook so it faces downward and slide the yarn through the loop. The loop on the hook should be kept loose enough so that the hook slides through easily.

chain

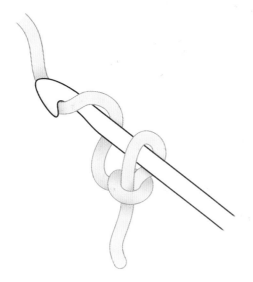

1. To create a chain, using the hook, yarn over hook, and pull it through the loop on the hook creating a new loop on the hook, yarn over hook again, and pull it through the loop on the hook.

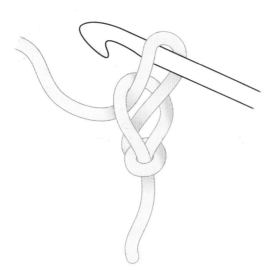

2. Continue in this way to create a chain. Keep moving your middle finger and thumb close to the hook to hold the work in place with the opposite hand that you hold your hook with.

chain ring/circle

If you are crocheting a round shape, one way of doing this is by crocheting a number of chains following the instructions in your pattern.

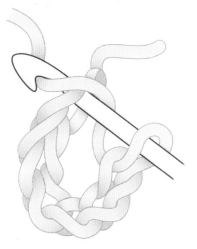

1. Join the chain into a circle by inserting the crochet hook into the first chain that you made (not into the slip knot), yarn over hook.

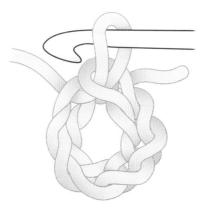

2. Pull the yarn through the chain and through the loop on your hook at the same time, thereby creating a slip stitch and forming a circle. You will now have a circle ready according to your pattern.

Most of the circles in this book have been made by creating a spiral, whereby you make two chains and insert your hook into the second chain from the hook (the first chain you made). Following the instructions in the pattern will then ensure the spiral has the correct amount of stitches. It's essential to use a marker stitch using this method, ensuring you know where to start and finish your round.

making rounds

Place a stitch marker at the beginning of each round; a piece of yarn in a contrasting color is useful for this. Loop the stitch marker into the first stitch and when you have made a round and reached the point where the stitch marker is, work this stitch, take out the stitch marker from the previous round, and put it back into the first stitch of the new round.

slip stitch

A slip stitch doesn't create any height and is often used as the last stitch in a row to create a smooth and even round.

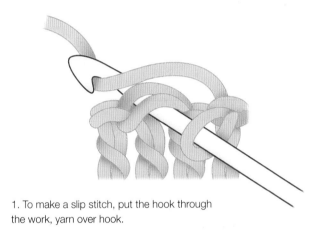

1. To make a slip stitch, put the hook through the work, yarn over hook.

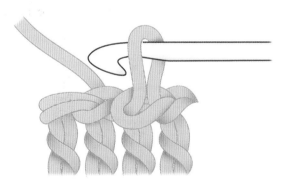

2. Pull the yarn through both the work and through the loop on the hook at the same time.

single crochet

1. Insert the hook into your work, yarn over hook and pull the yarn through the work so you have two loops on the hook.

2. Yarn over hook again and pull through the two loops on the hook. You will now have one loop on the hook.

half double

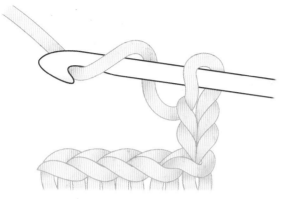

1. Before inserting the hook into the work, wrap the yarn over the hook and put the hook through the work with the yarn wrapped around.

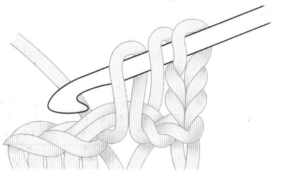

2. Yarn over hook again and pull through the first loop on the hook (you now have three loops on the hook).

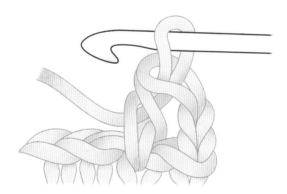

3. Pull yarn through all three loops. You'll be left with one loop on the hook.

double

1. Before inserting the hook into the work, wrap the yarn over the hook and put the hook through the work with the yarn wrapped around.

2. Yarn over hook again and pull through the first loop on the hook (you now have three loops on the hook). Yarn over hook again, pull the yarn through two loops (you now have two loops on the hook).

2. Pull the yarn through two loops again. You will be left with one loop on the hook.

making rows

When making straight rows you need to make a turning chain at the end to create the height you need for the stitch you're working with. To do this you just make the right number of chains for the stitch you are working in as follows:

Single crochet = 1 chain

Half double crochet = 2 chain

Double crochet = 3 chain

joining new yarn

If using single crochet, insert the hook as normal into the stitch using the original yarn and pull a loop through. Drop the old yarn and pick up the new yarn. Wrap new yarn over hook and pull it through the two loops on the hook.

increasing

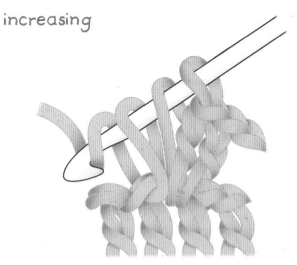

Make two stitches into one stitch from the previous row.

decreasing

You can decease by either missing the next stitch and continue crocheting, or by single crocheting two stitches together (sc2tog) as follows:

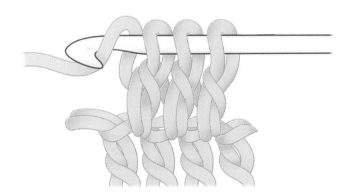

Insert the hook into your work, yarn over hook and pull the yarn through the work. You will now have two loops on the hook. Insert the hook into the next stitch, yarn over hook and pull the yarn through the work.

You will now have three loops on the hook, yarn over hook again and draw through all three loops on hook.

stuffing legs

If you want to make your toys stand up unsupported use plastic-coated wire when stuffing the legs. This technique is particularly useful as the wire is flexible and can be bent to position the toy in a variety of fun poses. To add the wire simply fold it in half, wrap with stuffing, then insert it into the toy. Make sure you fold the ends of the wire so that the sharp ends do not stick out of the toy. If you are making a toy for a baby or young children please do not use this technique, instead stuff the legs firmly.

templates

Buff-Orpington Chick's beak

See page 26

Buff-Orpington Chick's foot

See page 26

Buzz the Emu's foot

See page 80

Mrs Mittens' apron

See page 14

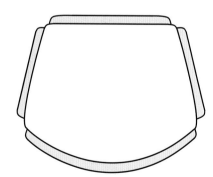

Vince the Spider's mouth

See page 85

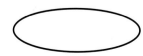

The Two Little Pigs' dress

See page 50

Pickle the Puppy's scarf

See page 52

NB: Enlarge by 130%

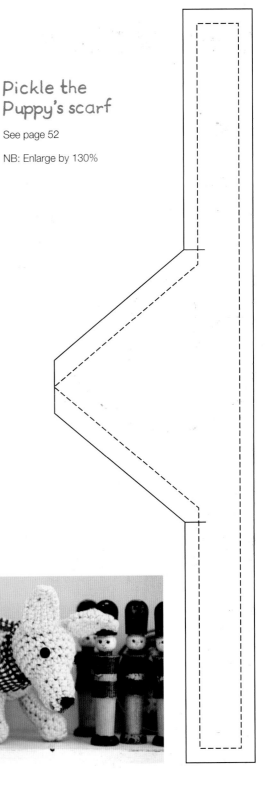

suppliers

The yarns used in these projects should be available from your local yarn or craft store. If you can't find the correct yarn try some of the websites listed here.

YARN SUPPLIERS

Adriafil Yarns
www.adriafil.com for stockists

Anny Blatt
www.annyblatt.com for stockists

Debbie Bliss
www.debbieblissonline.com

Bouton D'or
www.boutondor.com

Coats Craft Rowan Yarns
www.coatscrafts.co.uk

Colinette Yarns
www.colinette.com for stockists

Gedifra
Available from www.yarnmarket.com

Knitglobal
www.knitglobal.com

Lana Grossa
www.lanagrossa.com for stockists

Lanartus Yarns
www.lanartus.net

Lang Yarns
www.langyarns.ch/en

Louisa Harding
www.louisaharding.co.uk

Noro Yarns
www.noroyarns.com
for stockists

Patons Yarns
www.patonsyarns.co.uk

Presencia
www.presenciausa.com
for stockists

RY Classic Yarns
www.ryclassic.com

Sirdar Yarns
www.sirdar.co.uk

South West Trading Company (SWTC) Yarns
www.soysilk.com

Stef Francis
www.stef-francis.co.uk

Trendsetter Yarns
www.trendsetteryarns.com

Twilleys of Stamford
www.twilleys.co.uk for stockists

Wensleydale Longwool
www.wensleydalelongwoolsheepshop.co.uk

STOCKISTS

Knitting Fever
Stockists of Debbie Bliss, Noro, and Sirdar yarns
www.knittingfever.com

Knitting Garden
Stockists of Rowan yarns
www.theknittinggarden.com

Laughing Hens
Wool, patterns, knitting & crochet suppliers online
www.laughinghens.com

Lets Knit
www.letsknit.com

Unicorn Books and Crafts
www.unicornbooks.com

WEBS
www.yarn.com

Yarn Market
www.yarnmarket.com

TUITION

Nicki Trench Workshops
Crochet, knitting, and craft workshops all levels
Email: nicki@nickitrench.com

index

acknowledgments

The toys are all based on someone I know or a story I've heard from one of my family or friends, which makes them all the more special. My special thanks go to my daughters, Camilla and Maddy, who, though now teenagers, have embraced the toys as if they were still toddlers. Also, thanks to my mother, Beryl, who taught me to crochet and helped make the toys, and to David and Christopher, who joined me in having fun creating the characters. Particularly big thanks to Tracey Elks, who did a fantastic job at making the toys in time. And finally I'm very grateful to Cindy Richards for commissioning this book and to all involved at CICO for making the book happen.